MARKED BY
ECUADOR

MARKED BY ECUADOR

MIKE KRABAL

Marked by Ecuador
Copyright © 2021 by Mike Krabal

Printed in the United States of America

All rights reserved. No part of this publication may be reproduced, distributed, or transmitted in any form or by any means, including photocopying, recording, or other electronic or mechanical methods, without the prior written permission of the author and or publisher, except in the case of brief quotations embodied in critical reviews. Although every precaution has been taken in the preparation of this book, the author assumes no responsibility for errors or omissions. Some names and identifying details have been changed to protect the privacy of individuals.

If you wish to communicate with Mike Krabal, you may reach him at mikekrabal.com.

ISBN   978-0-9975800-3-7

Thank You

To those that hosted me in a foreign country, thank you for keeping me safe and allowing me to return home with stories. Thank you for sharing your homes, feeding me, and helping me grow as a person. I now know hospitality is infinite.

Contents

Introduction	1
Getting There	7
Foreign Discoveries	27
A Family Christmas	49
Mamita Building and Macas	65
Genuine Ecuador	75
Into the Amazon	97
To Civilization	119
Baños and the Bus	129
Guayaquil and the Girls and the Beach and the Birds	141
Return to Vilcabamba	157
Saraguro and Cuenca	165
Two Friends and a Redemption	179
Carnival	193
Three Months as a Foreigner	207

Introduction

I'm as qualified to leave West Virginia's hills for a South American country as I am to lead a mission to Mars. After a few years of working with Latinos in pizza joints, I picked up some Spanish curse words. Way back in high school Spanish, I learned how to count in another language—uno; dos; tres; cuatro; cinco; seis. As an unstable thirty-five-year-old, I had little more to offer Ecuadorians than a touristy, navy-blue set of squinting eyeballs.

I went to Ecuador anyway. That's become my style: ditch the rat race, listen to my heart, and take a magic carpet ride powered by curiosity and born of chance. Five years earlier, I had spent four months roaming the United States on my motorcycle. That ride was inspired by a chance encounter with an eighty-one-year-old woman who told me I should get out more. It was an adventure big enough to give me the balls to do something similar later in life. But I didn't know when, or if it that inspiration would ever strike again.

Yet, it did. And nearly in the same way. The notion of chance once again entered my life. It stuck two invisible hands on my shoulders, looked me in the eye, and said, "Mike, you're in for it. You're about to meet another woman aged well into her wisdom years. She's going to change your life. The last one turned you into a writer. This one's going to turn you into a foreigner."

In the summer of 2015, I had a chance encounter with a sixty-eight-year-old motorcyclist at an ice cream parlor. Her name was Emily. She and I formed a hand-dipped friendship based on our shared love of adventuring by motorcycle. Through Emily, another friendship formed with Alice—her equally fascinating sister. Emily described Alice as someone who was a fellow writer. She said her sister was fluent in four languages and had lived in multiple countries. Alice was also trained in voice dialogue, a type of therapy that could have done me a whole lot of good, according to Emily. Over a few lunches, Emily intuited that I was like a sticky fly trap of collected issues. She believed her sister could straighten me out. The trouble was; Alice spent most of her time 3000 miles south of West Virginia; in Ecuador. Many months would pass before I'd meet her.

When that opportunity came, Alice traveled to the US to rehab a property she owned in my county. She needed the property repaired and remodeled so that she could sell it. Emily negotiated a deal between Alice and me where I'd trade labor for voice dialogue sessions.

When Alice and I met, I had arrived at her property for a day's work. In her gravel driveway, I parked and stared through my truck's windshield. If a heart could groan, mine would have. The place looked incredibly repelling. I knew little of its backstory and had no interest in getting involved with a building in such a state. My patience went from plenty to thin before I'd even stepped out of the truck.

I'd earned a strong distaste for construction work due to how I became good at it. I call it the poor-man's paradigm. It's life experience earned through fixing broken things with your own two hands and sheer determination. A person gains those skills because they can't afford to pay anyone to do things for them. It's a lifestyle where you reach working age and often hear the term 'good money.' To a blue-collar grunt, good money means a salary that pays the bills while never getting a hair further than paycheck-to-paycheck. Construction jobs lured me with good money right out of high school. But, by my mid-thirties, I knew myself as more of a wanna-be writer than a swinger of the hammer. Construction work simply never supplied the satisfaction I hoped for.

No matter which way you shake it, life had given me the skills to help Alice. Those years in construction imprinted the ability to look at something and know the extent of a job nearly instantly. Alice's place was like being up against the ropes and too tired to swing. A pipe had burst and flooded the entire bottom floor the previous winter. Consequently, mold had taken over the house in her absence. The first floor had been completely gutted to deal with the mold. Since I was working full time, I knew getting involved in her project would mean the elimination of my weekends and evenings for the next thousand years.

Alice was in a pinch. That was easily understood. Through my eyes, her offering me therapy wasn't as valuable as the repairs I'd make. To tell the truth, I wasn't at all interested in the therapy. Me and my problems had cohabited for thirty-five years without being arrested. It's fair to say that I could have smoothly continued without therapy; though, Alice's fascinating life made me want to be her friend. I wanted to hear her stories and learn from her. I didn't want anything else—especially side work.

Since I'd arrived on the property, I decided to live up to my word. Instead of construction, she had me pull weeds. I pulled a million weeds. Her entire yard was a weed. It needed regular mowing and grass seed rather than plucking each individual plant out of the yard. All the while, she wanted me to reference pulling the weeds out of my mind in preparation for the voice dialogue session later that day. This, I thought, was pure silliness. Being our first time around one another, Alice was freaking me out a bit.

She was eccentric. She had an unwavering optimism concerning the job at hand. She said of it, "It will be fun!" After grinding through thousands of hours of manual labor, I never felt like I was having fun. Now, give me a shot of whiskey, a good tune, and a cute brunette. I'll tell you all about fun. The repairs needed at Alice's had fun written nowhere on them.

So, I ducked out on Alice halfway through the day. I went for lunch and never returned. They call it ghosting these days. I felt sorry for her and ashamed for what I'd done. I was sure I wasn't the guy who was going to remodel the whole place. Many local contractors needed and wanted that kind of work. *Why not give it to them,* I thought. I cut the strand of our friendship in half, not caring if it would continue.

Fortunately, Alice was one hell of a mender. She never gave up on me. She saw an opportunity to help someone and cared to follow through. But I didn't allow it. I really didn't want any part of her remodel. I dodged each request for help until she returned to Ecuador. We remained in the slimmest of contact over the next half year.

In October of 2016, she was back in the States. She had secured some construction help via the internet and local connections while she was away. Her return brought an exchange of long emails. These were absolutely saturated with her robust optimism, so much so that our friendship repaired itself. And, all the while, her remodeling crept along. I became more confident that I could help at the tail end of her project.

Between October and December, I spent all of my free time doing the exact same thing I bitched about earlier. I repaired decking boards, laid floor tile, built an enclosure around her hot water heater, trimmed, and painted until I was blue in the face. I ran new wiring and carried every last object from the house to a storage building on another part of the property. I even excavated and installed a new septic line. In mid-November, it became clear to me, in an instant, why I'd been doing this. It was for far more than therapy.

One afternoon, I was in the bathroom painting one of the corners a teal color. The brush went up. The brush went down. I'd dip the brush, and I'd stroke. I'd dip, and I'd stroke. Rather mindless, it was. Then a moment came when my gut's mind got involved. Like a shot of liquor and a pelvic thrust into a taser, a surge of warmth and electricity cloaked my abdomen the exact moment I was struck with the thought, "I bet she'd let me go to Ecuador with her!" I mean, it was tangible. The feeling was knowing that everything was going to work out.

I laid the brush down, hooked a right out of the bathroom, and went straight to Alice. Somewhat grinning, I asked, "Can I go to Ecuador with you?" She replied, "Absolutely!" She said it so quickly that it was like her tongue had been waiting for the question.

Later that evening, I searched for a flight. There were none available in my price range, however, where I could've flown to Ecuador with Alice. So, I would have to leave two weeks later on my own. During that time, I tightened up all the loose ends at her property to make it sellable. She and I agreed that, upon her receiving the free construction labor, she would provide me a room at her place where I could stay. Moreover, I learned that Americans traveling to Ecuador for more than ninety days would need to purchase a $450 travel Visa. I hadn't the money for that. So, I paid for my flights and committed to being a ninety-day foreigner with $579 to my name

Getting There
December 8, 2016

In all fairness, my first thought regarding my last day in America was, "Oh shit." Over and over, that thought recurred while traveling to Ecuador. I'd begin the journey at Dulles International Airport in Northern Virginia. From there, I'd fly to Houston, where I had a twenty-one-hour layover. A twenty-one hour layover is enough to fry the brain of a frustrated, regular traveler. Though, for me, it couldn't have been long enough.

In fact, it was good news. Some of my best friends lived near Houston, so I'd have a chance to see them. I'd be plenty far away from home to feel as though I'm traveling while easing into this rather large commitment of time. I liked it that way. To feel blasted into highly unfamiliar circumstances was no longer as welcomed by my nature as it used to be.

I'm one to do things, being that I'll blindly commit to just about anything. If you'd ask, "Hey Mike do you wanna go skydiving right now?" My response would be a quick yes. But I'm not one to be overly stoked in the moment of participation. Years have shown me that I'm happy for having done things. I find myself proud to have had the grit to move forward. Still, I'm rarely the type who would high-five you and say, "Hell yeah, man! We're going to Ecuador!" Instead, I'm the type of person who secretly hopes to have a good time while returning home with all of my limbs. That's just me. I'm a first-born. I'm a big brother. I'm close to my parents. I've grown more cautious. I'm a wanna-be. I wanna be cool and relaxed all the time, even if it's impossible.

On the day of departure to Ecuador, I purposely tried not to think about the commitment looming at 5:39 p.m. That's when the plane would leave my comfortable country and comfort zone behind for a midnight arrival in Ecuador's capital city of Quito. When I would prefer a day to drag on, of course, it flew by among friends, laughs, and good Texan food.

At Houston's George Bush Intercontinental Airport, 5:39 p.m. came as reliably as it does every day. I was sitting on the plane thinking, *Here we go! This trip just got real!* There were a hundred other people on the plane looking like they were thinking, *This is going to take forever.* They looked bored the moment they sat in their seats. Within ten minutes of takeoff, I swear thirty percent of them were asleep.

Anxiety was pulsating from my toes to my temple. I was in an aisle seat. Beside me, a pretty Latina was hacking her lungs up like she was going to get a trophy for it. A Canadian woman sat in the window seat. She'd later describe her only other time in Ecuador as terrifying.

In the spring of 2016, I lost my spleen in a motorcycle crash. The spleen is the body's immune-system organ. The Latina's hackathon had me convinced I'd show up in South America with a case of chickenpox gone wild. Her sneezes were as powerful as toilet flushes. Her nose was a faucet of snot. There were tissues containing more mucus than paper within reach. I was sure I'd catch it. And, I was sure that nobody could cure it.

Halfway through the flight, the Canadian woman shared a story with the sick Latina and me. With great conviction, she told us of her first time in Ecuador. She had been out drinking in Quito. She was on her own and had met some locals. During the night, someone had slipped a roofie into her drink. The next day, she awoke somewhere in the city, not knowing how she got there or who she was with at the time. I absorbed this information as if my life depended on it.

Like a breeding ground for paranoia, her story did nothing to ease my mind about going to another country. Sarcastically, I thanked her for the hours of pondering the uncertainty ahead as we flew through the night sky directly toward the city where she was roofied.

It was exactly midnight when we landed in Quito. I was still awake. Outside, the view from the plane was mysterious. I was in South America. It was hard to believe. Flying there in the darkness of night made it seem as if it wasn't confirmed that we were in Ecuador. We certainly had landed in Quito, but there was no sense of the distance traveled. Rather, there was only an awareness of time spent sitting in an aisle seat, looking around at dark windows.

When it came time to leave the plane, I was dreading the move. My oh my, my comfort zone felt millions of miles away. When I reached for words to think, once again, "Oh shit." was all I had. Entering the airport as a solo-traveling red-headed white guy, I was sure I'd be targeted for crime. I was nearly dizzy with anxiety. Americans come up missing all the time in foreign countries. And I had just thrust myself into a situation where the odds of that happening increased.

No longer was I at home and telling friends, "Hey, man, I'm going to Ecuador for the winter." In which case, they'd share their surprise, enthusiasm, and well wishes. Sure, it felt kind of cool saying it while I was in West Virginia. Now, being in Quito, I had to face the music. Suddenly, the coolness had vanished. I felt like a pud. I was there, and backing out was impossible. The only option was to move forward. With each step toward the terminal, I was looking for whoever would pick my pocket, just like the Canadian woman had warned. I was adrenalized—whipping my head in any direction from which any noise came.

Embarrassingly, if I was a superhero, my name would be Caution Man. My superpower would be the ability to watch out! And my cape would be day-glow green. I really like feeling safe, but I put myself in harm's way, nonetheless, for the sake of fending off a life lived regrettably. And that's the very definition of bravery.

Leaving the plane was followed by a passport

screening and customs. After a short wait, I found myself in front of a female customs officer. She asked a few questions while my passport was in her hand. Seemingly convinced, she stamped it. I went to gather my luggage and to join the others in a customs security line.

Off to my right, officers, clad in green camo, were sifting through bags. This line barely moved. I had brought nothing of importance to worry about—only clothes, my camera gear, a laptop, a few books, and some grocery items Alice had requested. She had said a few things were hard to find in Ecuadorian markets.

The security check should have been a breeze. Oddly, I had been in line a half hour when an officer detached the queue line strap and ushered me through a door away from the security check. An "Oh shit." popped in my head, as I'd seen no other traveler pulled from the line and directed through that door. *Here we go! Time for the full-body search.* But I was completely wrong. That door led directly to the terminal. The officer had expedited the process. Why? I have no idea. My bags didn't get searched.

I found a seat in the terminal. My next flight was scheduled for six a.m. Once I calmed and could think like a human again, I noticed how the airport was up to par with any airport. It was quite nice. Every aspect was modern, clean, and normal feeling. Overall, it was a fraction of the size of the United States' mega airports. Quito's airport was more like a supremely well-built regional airport.

People shuffled outside toward taxis. Families were welcoming their arrivals. It was quiet and peaceful in the way I had experienced other airports being. They're kind of like libraries. For those waiting on a connecting flight, they're a host to unhurried browsing and sitting in silence. I had nothing to do but wait.

Somewhere around two a.m., I found a spot in an unpopulated corner of the airport. I laid on the floor for a nap. I kept one arm on my suitcase and used my backpack as a pillow. My heightened state of alarm wouldn't fade enough to sleep. I laid there, eyes closed, trying to relax. Here and there, I'd hear feet shuffling by. I'd open my eyes to read the situation. It was just another peaceful passerby. I'd hear an unfamiliar message come out of the intercom, and I'd listen. My instinct was to pay attention to everything, even with my eyes closed.

Near four a.m., I heard a voice. It was a male voice and in English. I was really beginning to get drowsy, so I left my eyes closed and pretended not to hear it. I wasn't sure the person was speaking to me, anyway. Moments later, the silence was interrupted again. "Hey man," said the voice. I opened my eyes to see an Ecuadorian man sitting on the floor twenty-feet away. He was holding a lean angle in my direction. He was smiling at me. I sat upright to greet him. "Hey," I replied.

His name was Luis. He was caught in thick boredom by the stillness of the airport. I took this as an opportunity to get to know the country I was visiting. Luis was a native of Ecuador but had spent most of his adult years working in the States. Minus an accent, his English was spot on. He was curious as to why I was in Ecuador. I obliged his curiosity and matched his questions with questions. He told of his adventures working in the US. He told me of his hurdles in learning English and of his son's move to the US. He was proud to tell me of the elevator repair job that his son found once he was in the States. I told him how it had been traveling the past two days and of my concerns for the day of travel to come. For the next two hours, I was in good company and gave worrying a break.

It was six a.m., and I had been awake for twenty-two hours. I was part of a group of nearly fifty travelers who were shuttled to a large propeller-powered Tame airplane. This was a first for me. I knew that we would downgrade from a large commercial passenger aircraft to fly into Southern Ecuador. But a propeller-powered airplane wasn't what I'd imagined.

The shuttle dropped us off in the staging area of a runway. The plane had a ramp leading to it, the type you'd see a president step out of while he's waving at a crowd of onlookers. The first light of day illuminated an enormous mountain range running parallel to the runway. These were the tallest mountains I'd seen. They looked like the Rockies without snow. These were the giant, green Andes. They were responsible for Quito's elevation of 9,350 feet.

We climbed the steps and took our seats inside. The plane was headed south to Catamayo, Ecuador. The flight would only be an hour. While flying, I was looking out the window and dozed off. When I awoke, seconds or maybe minutes later, I was flabbergasted. I whispered, "Where am I? And, why, the hell, am I on a plane?" Out the window, giant, mystical mountain peaks soared into the sky. They looked like steep islands poking through a sea of cotton ball clouds. Inside the plane, no one looked familiar. I was soaked in sweat. My short-term memory had been wiped clean. When things began to clear up, the anxiety once again reared its unwanted head.

Soon, the world outside became blessed by an expansive blue sky. The Andes, below, had taken on a caramel color tone. Between those peaks, a flat, jigsaw puzzle of green farmland created a valley floor. Here, the mountains rose directly to the sky without notable foothills. The pilot initiated a hard right turn, beginning our descent into the lower portion of the valley.

The mountain tops now bested our cruising altitude. From a couple hundred feet in the air, I could see rudimentary-looking homes spreading through the farmland. This was my first view of rural Ecuadorian life. Then, I spotted Catamayo's airport runway.

We landed safely, and I fell in line like a sheep here. I followed everyone out of the plane, down another flight of portable steps, and toward the terminal. There was no ignoring the excitement born from the surrounding terrain. It was stunning. For the second time in little more than an hour, I'd say to myself, "These are the biggest mountains I've seen." Walking to the terminal, my neck was cranked hard to the right as I stared at the mountains.

Catamayo's terminal was much smaller than Quito's. Inside, a tiny U-shaped baggage claim conveyor brought us our things. It looked like a long grocery-checkout conveyor with a curve. With bags in hand, I'd have to begin negotiating my way to Alice's farm in Vilcabamba, Ecuador—two and a half hours south.

Alice had given me a very specific set of instructions written in Spanish. I released them from my pocket and exited the rear of the terminal. Just as she had said, there were taxi drivers ready to swarm me. She said to sternly dictate where I needed to go while offering them how much I was willing to pay. She meant that I'd say these things, in Spanish, of course. Goal number one was to get myself to the bus terminal in Catamayo. My lack of confidence for this going smoothly literally had me shaking.

Six men approached me. They were speaking Spanish so fast that it might as well have been Pentecostal tongues. I looked down at my sheet of instructions and began to verbally butcher the Spanish sentences. I formed the words so slowly that a gray-haired taxi driver stepped forward, yanking the paper right out of my hand. Meanwhile, the other men were trying to attract my business with rapid phrases and gestures. I was overwhelmed.

Within the confusion, the old taxi driver stood out as the option to whom I was going to commit. He began eagerly motioning me toward his cab while offering to carry my bags. I was so on guard that I had a white-knuckle grip on their handles. I plainly wasn't going to hand them over. Years of negative news stories, and incidences shared by friends, took forward space in my mind. I was now dealing with foreigners on their turf. I knew the rule of law was different here. I was unfamiliar with any road I'd travel. And I was aware of the stereotype held by some of the world's population. Theoretically, all Americans are wealthy—and perhaps worth a ransom. I mention these things because the driver was now completely ignoring my request to be taken to Catamayo's bus terminal.

For just that instant that he held my instructions in his hand, he noticed where I was ultimately headed. He had recognized an opportunity to take advantage of my brand-new-to-Ecuador status. He sensed my concerned, present nature. He knew he had me.

We left in his car with me repeating my request, "El terminal de bus. Catamayo." He'd reply with a sarcastic look in the rear-view mirror and a giant, gotcha smile accompanying the question "A Loja?" (To Loja). This happened a dozen times. He knew that taking me to Catamayo's bus terminal would earn him two dollars in American money. But if he could get me further down the road to Loja, he could charge twenty. My Spanish was as good as a noodle for kite string. Negotiation was off the table. I evaluated the situation.

I was relatively safe. Despite his multiple attempts to pick up other riders that I thwarted, it was just me and him in the cab. I could handle things as long as we stayed on the general course. The thought of getting on a public bus in a foreign country really wasn't any more appealing to me than being duped by this guy in the taxi. I had experienced several Greyhound terminals in America that were alarmingly sketchy. I couldn't imagine Ecuador's terminals being better than those. We had an hour's drive to Loja. I decided to no longer make it an issue.

Here and there, he'd try to initiate conversation. I was incapable of comprehension. I'd shrug my shoulders and mumble something in English. He'd get the point, shake his head and smile, and refocus on the road. Out the cab's windows, we had climbed over a remarkable mountain pass. In the highest of elevations, there were conifers with soft, long needles that hung off branch ends like a horse's mane. It was a land of fantastic beauty. In the moments where he wasn't trying to make a ballsy pass on the car ahead of him, I rode along full of stomach butterflies and in utter wonder. No place I'd been had ever quite looked like this place. It was almost immediately evident that I was cruising through the most beautiful terrain of my life.

Steep, mountain farmland soon gave way to urbanism. We descended into a city that I assumed was Loja. There was a sprawling landscape of mountains densely decorated with homes. My short time in California, years before, came to mind. At first glance, Loja's arrangement looked like a Beverly Hills full of smaller homes and Latin influence. The build quality of the houses was only slightly subpar to first-world homes. Right away, I noticed the Ecuadorian's prolific use of concrete in their building strategy. I put the brakes on that observation as we pulled into Loja's bus terminal.

Knowing that I was heading to Vilcabamba, the taxi driver made a last-minute push to continue driving me there. He had dollar signs in his eyes. Repeatedly, he asked, in Spanish, "To Vilcabamba? To Vilcabamba?" And to each, "To Vilcabamba," I'd reply with a stern, "No!" By now, I'd learned that he was only after my money. Yet, he was just honest enough to take me in the direction I was going. I paid him his shadily earned twenty and left the cab in the throes of growing anxiety.

In Loja's bus terminal, two voices were in my mind.

There was Alice's voice of instruction. It was a reminder of the exact moves that needed to be made to efficiently make it through the terminal. She told me where I'd enter the building, where I'd exit for the bus, which bus company to use, what color their buses were, and where their ticket window was located. Many transportation companies share the same bus terminals in Ecuador. They're arranged as adjacent offices behind large panes of glass. Alice told me that I'd have to secure an American dime to work the turnstile at the building's exit. She left no stone unturned. That was her voice in my head.

Then there was the voice of roofie girl. She had told me of being pickpocketed in bus terminals. She told me, "Watch your back. They can be rough places." That was enough to peg my anxiety right off of the top of the meter. Naturally, her voice plowed through to the forefront of my thoughts.

I entered the heavily populated terminal on high alert. I felt like Mr. Minority, Mr.-target-on-his-back, Mr.-highly-outnumbered-rich-American, and Mr.-I-hope-I-don't-have-to-defend-myself. Knowing my fighting prowess well, I had no illusions of being Chuck Norris. I had no inner belief that I could whoop a handful of pocket-picking Ecuadorians with a series of swift kicks and chops to their jugulars. All the same, roofie girl's story did no favors for me. The time in Loja's terminal was the single greatest moment of disabling anxiety I'd felt in my life. My brain practically shut down.

I'd forgotten Alice's instructions. I couldn't remember where the service window was for the bus company I needed. I could neither remember the name of the company nor remember the color of the buses. This forced me to walk both floors and search for it. I put on my best I-know-what-I'm-doing-face and quickened my stride. I was indeed a foreigner far off my beaten path. At six-foot-one and as pale as a bowl of sugar, I was catching glances. *What are they thinking? Who's gonna make a move?* Instinctual thoughts dominated me. I was insanely, irrationally guarded.

In time, I found the window for the bus company servicing Vilcabamba. It was called Vilcaturis. I had my backpack and luggage bag so tightly gripped that I didn't want to let go of them to reach into my pocket for money. When I did go for my front pocket, I looked around first to see who was looking. This felt like being a drug-dealer and scoping the scene for cops. To the girl in the window, my mannerisms may have been the sketchiest thing she'd seen in a while.

My front pockets were everything to me. My now $559 was there. My passport was there, as were my IDs. Just reaching for my pocket was a dead giveaway to the goods.

Nonetheless, I secured a ticket. At the exiting turnstile, I went for the wrong lane. So, I was directed by a uniformed employee to take another lane. I couldn't decipher his Spanish command and repeatedly attempted to proceed through. The employee adjusted the command and added gestures. I got the message. The turnstile I was trying to use was out of service.

Behind the terminal, I spotted the bus. I showed the porter my ticket and took a seat among the others. I was an absolute nervous wreck. Minus the micro-nap on the flight to Catamayo, I'd been awake and on high-alert for twenty-five hours. Vilcabamba was an hour and a half further south.

The bus was loaded with an ordinary mixture of old and young folks. It was not the scene I'd imagined beforehand. It wasn't full of hardened criminals who'd pile in the seats directly around me. It wasn't a scene where the biggest one would sit in my seat beside me and stare me down. There wasn't anyone willing to sit with me while wielding the knife that was meant to be plunged in my side. Still, my guard remained high.

Lurching out of the terminal, I noticed the bus had a manual transmission. This caught me as quite novel in the moment. I experienced a brief, positive emotional swing. I'd never even heard of a full-sized passenger bus with a manual transmission. The bus was also adorned with logos and decals to give it some enthusiastic spice. These were welcomed momentary distractions.

From the terminal, we wandered deeper into Loja. This was a city with a business on every corner and two in between. It seemed a rather thick collage of residential and entrepreneurial. The hours of being awake, as well as fueled on adrenaline, were really starting to take their toll. Passing through the city, I realized that I could be more proactive in recording the journey despite the fear of exposing my electronics. I was without a smartphone at this point in my life. Call me a late bloomer. I had brought along a cheap Sony Handycam and a decent Canon camera. I took the Handycam out of my backpack. I swiveled my neck around to see who was watching me. It seemed as if I was in the clear, so I held my camera nearly against the bus window. I also held it low enough so that the other passengers wouldn't see what I was doing.

Loja was intriguing. Buildings were painted every color under the sun. Some structures held the mark of Spanish colonialism, and some looked like ideas come to life. Logos and businesses I'd never heard of were everywhere. The cars, trucks, and motorcycles were unrecognizable. I enjoyed passing through Loja's variety-laden streets. I wanted to capture it on video. Who knew if I'd see the place again?

The bus climbed up and out of Loja's Cuxibamba Valley and away from the city. The Andes were intensely green here. They were extremely steep, and worth repeating, intensely green. Agricultural ventures had taken much of the forest, leaving heavenly meadows as breathtaking side effects. Now and then, we'd pass a shack-like home perched on a sliver of land between the road and a precarious mountainside. Sometimes, there would be people outside. They were deeply rural folks—mountain farmers. As the bus twisted and groaned through the hills and corners, I was struck by the magnificence so much that it was like the landscape could, in itself, sedate my anxiety. I became a little braver displaying my video camera.

Though, I wasn't quite as brave as the bus driver. The rules of the road seemed to be that were not any rules to the road. If that driver could leave the bus in a gear long enough to reach high rpm, he'd go for a pass. He'd pass on a downhill, an uphill, going into a corner, or coming out. He'd pass anywhere. I thought it rather amusing, given my eighteen years of motorcycle racing. It almost sounds crazy saying that his driving didn't bother me much after expressing the crippling anxiety felt in the bus terminal. Somewhere there's a deep imbalance in practical confidence in my being. In any case, I'd be lying if I said I hadn't left a little space in my mind for the thought of our bus barrel rolling off of a cliff. That's what the American media portrays of foreign mountain roads and passenger buses.

Along the route, we'd stop in a couple towns. All were magnificently beautiful, and all were mountain towns. People would get on. People would get off. We'd pick up hitchhikers and drop them off at their homes. I would get a couple looks, here and there. And, by golly, the looks were friendly.

When we crossed the last mountain pass into Vilcabamba, I might as well have been in heaven. It was a green world of sheer peaks, rock formations, and farmland. We pulled into the bus terminal. I was nearing twenty-seven hours awake since I'd been in Houston. When I exited the bus and spotted Alice, the leaden weight of anxiety left my shoulders. I felt light again. I felt completely safe again. I nearly teared up with joy as the worry left my body. Seeing her meant I'd made it.

Vilcabamba was to be my nearest taste of civilization. It was where I thought Alice lived. But she didn't live in town. Nor would I. There were still five miles to cover before I'd ultimately reach my destination. Alice needed a few moments to walk through town and purchase some things. When she was finished, we searched for a taxi to head to her place.

She hailed a pickup truck taxi. It was a small, green, and white diesel pickup truck. As far as I knew, there were no small diesel pickup trucks in the US. Volkswagon sold diesel cars in the US, but not pickups. I wasn't for sure why. Here in Vilcabamba, these diesel pickup taxis were plentiful. We jumped in the bed of one of them and headed out of town.

We drove a short distance on a painted-line road, then made a turn onto an unmarked road. We were headed toward another mountain valley and her neck of the woods. She lived on a couple-hundred-acre property that was half mountainside, half non-commercial farm. It had been necessary for Alice to meet me in Vilcabamba, as rural Ecuadorian homes generally didn't have addresses. I wouldn't have known what to tell a taxi driver to get to her place.

On the unmarked road, twisty turns matched the fast-rushing Vilcabamba River. Plants grew thick and tall here—right up to the edge of the road. Tiny clusters of homes, some sturdy and some fairly weathered, popped up now and then. There were dogs and chickens and children around these homes. I noticed makeshift stores of the type that's really someone's home and doubles as a market.

We were dropped off at the head of a gravel road. *This must be where Alice drives to her place.* We started walking down the road. On the right, there was a clearing, a few ultra-rudimentary covered benches, and a dirt patch used as a volleyball court. But there was no car. Twenty yards ahead flowed the Vilcabamba River. As we rounded a turn just a bit more, I saw a suspended walk bridge over the river. Alice headed for it. I followed with a grin on my face.

The bridge was steel with rusted diamond-plate

panels for traction. Two thick, steel-braided cables provided the strength for the bridge and made for handrails. On each riverbank, heavy concrete pillars served as attachment points for the cables. When we walked across, the bridge reacted with a light sway, like the feeling of standing on a boat in mildly choppy water.

Stepping off the bridge, we ascended a dirt path lined with encroaching, thick, green foliage. This path was a remnant of a road. I followed Alice, step for step, with no idea how far we'd walk to arrive at her property. Given that we had to cross a suspended walk bridge, and now we were hiking a dirt path to her place, I felt oddly adventurous. *How far are we going,* I wondered.

The answer came around a bend and about seventy yards from the walk bridge. On our right was an elaborate stone gate with a terracotta, decorative roof. It had rod iron bars, artfully fashioned into a giant butterfly. We had arrived at Alice's.

Getting in required unlocking the gate with a key. On either side of the gate, thick vegetation and large boulders blocked access from simply slipping around it. A few yards away, Alice's home sat waiting for our arrival—as did her husband Dan. He welcomed me to their place with a smile and something to the effect of, "Nice to finally meet you." Dan and I had engaged a few times via Facebook before my arrival.

My hosts were highly educated in the world of academia, and potentially more so, in the world of earned experience as they were in their early seventies. They were supremely in tune in the ways and happenings of the Earth. Both had done a few laps around the big blue globe in their time. Dan had a science background with an affinity for high-grade technology. He was an accomplished musician and an artist supremely attuned to the colors and patterns developed naturally in biology. He had proudly mastered ROLFing—a form of physical therapy. It is massage-like in nature, and used for the anatomical realignment of a body by way of manipulating its tightened muscle fascia.

Alice was a jill of all trades if those trades were of intellect and interest. She was a published author and a champion of world and local environmental care. She lived by the mantra, "Leave the trail better than you found it." She was a solution-based individual in a world full of problem-focused peers. And, like me, she had practical knowledge in the construction of homes.

The next three months were sure to be ones of learning and growth. I had always desired to be in the company of folks who had been there and done that far more than myself. Now, I had traveled to Ecuador to bunker down with two perfect examples of this. I perceived them as good company from whom I could learn and with whom I could explore Ecuador. But I was exhuasted. With good intention, I had to find a way to get away from them long enough to take a nap. It had been twenty-nine hours awake.

Foreign Discoveries

Throughout the world, there are places where the planet is arranged so that the inhabitants of that area benefit. For their psyche, the natural beauty may be so that people are calmed when they absorb it. For safety, these places may provide isolation from an outside world rampaging along a course of pollution and disassociation birthed from technology. For health, the weather may be so optimal that the fortunate inhabitants spend a thicker slice of time recreating in the sun and moving their bodies. For social wealth, these places may host a culture where family still matters and still gathers. This combination of gifts may provide greater vitality to the residents who've collected the most years on this planet.

    Some folks are lucky enough to be born in such places. Some are lucky to find such a place. It's thought that this sort of collective experience affords the elderly citizens of Vilcabamba a position of greater vitality than most places on planet Earth. They're the beneficiaries of the Ecuadorian environment, healthy foods, and strong family ties. Vilcabamba is a tiny Andean town littered with exceptionally healthy, long-lived folks.

It's a treasure of a place. At 5000 feet, its elevation rarely lets the temperature get more than a stone's throw away from seventy degrees. It's a place with a dry season and a wet season. More so, it's a place locked in what some call perpetual springtime. Both seasons share half of the year's calendar. Its equatorial location grants it the possibility of gorgeous sunrises and sunsets at nearly 6:30 a.m. and 6:30 p.m. each day of the year. Ecuador's summer and winter solstices have but a tiny four-minute difference.

The mountains really make Vilcabamba what it is. I can say the same for my home. Mountains really make West Virginia what it is. Mountains really make Colorado what it is. On and on, the benefits of clean air and a simple and purposeful existence are often found in mountainous regions.

In the land around Vilcabamba, there are crisp mountain springs and creek-sized rivers flowing with liquid gold—at least that's how many of the residents like to think of it. Many speculate that the region's water is an additional secret to their longevity. And now, on a worldwide stage, Vilcabamba's water is getting recognition for its mineral content. Have the residents homed in on the fountain of youth? Are the surrounding mountains the fountain? One couldn't know without spending the better part of a lifetime drinking it.

My interest in Ecuador, and especially Vilcabamba, began like a baby crawling. Alice would constantly mention the place while she was in the States. I listened lightly. I just couldn't think such a place still existed. *Surely, we would've ruined it by now.* But my interest bolted upright and started running when I was virtually introduced to Vilcabamba through a sixteen-minute YouTube video. It was a video of the type that sells a place.

In the video, a calming female voice narrated as slow, panning shots sifted through green foliage, and allowed sunrays to own the lens for the slightest of moments. Footage of children playing freely, near a fountain in the town's square, brought to mind more innocent times. Relaxed faces matched the relaxed-looking, colorful buildings of the town. The video's mention of the water and the area's old-timey, sugar cane operations sparked more curiosity. A giant rock formation named Mandango was shown. It sat as a guardian above the town. Watching the video was the first time I'd heard about the resident's claimed longevity.

Sure, Vilcabamba's funny name initiated an internal singing of "La Bamba" by Ritchie Valens. But after watching that video a dozen times, I had to go see Vilcabamba for myself. I wanted to see if a place really existed that could live up to a video edited to portray a near paradise.

The previous day when I stepped off the bus to meet Alice, a world of surprises began playing on my senses. I started noticing things I'd seen in the video. There was a well-worn, wooden cane press outside of a corner market. Alice and I stopped for a drink of cane juice. It was the first natural thing I ingested as a foreigner. It was as green as juiced kale but smooth and naturally sweet. While drinking it, I thought I'd have to watch ingesting raw foods. But that worry was somewhat trivial in the moment. We finished our drinks and ventured onward.

Since she'd come to meet me, she was making good use of her time in Vilcabamba. She wanted to restock the basics. I followed her in innocent wonder. *"Right over there is the town square and its blue cathedral. Oh, and right there is that fountain! And there are kids playing around it, just like in the video."* Then I thought, *There's Mandango!* I'd seen it on the bus coming into town, though I could really train my eyes upon it on foot. *I want to climb it. Look at this place!*

Alice was all business as she roamed about. She'd say, "This place has really great bread." Or, "This is where we get our milk." And I'd think, "It's all in the same gigantic grocery store back home." Here, there were still specialists: bakers, cheese makers, organic farmers—not just corporate food shipped in on trucks.

Sometimes, Alice would stop and speak with someone. We met a white woman from Virginia. There was an Ecuadorian man. Alice could switch from English to Spanish like she had a toggle on her tongue. It didn't matter who we met. It seemed as if she could respond with a language to match. We met a young, shirtless, traveling-sort from Eastern Europe who had been in Vilcabamba for several months. Alice probably knew how to speak to him since she knew Russian; however, he chose to engage us in English.

Vilcabamba's chill lifestyle has gained world attention as a prime place to exist. It's a magnet for earthly wanderers—hippies, some call them.

I wouldn't get to know Vilcabamba right away. There were some aspects of staying with Alice on which I didn't have a grasp. Before I came, I didn't realize there was a five-mile barrier between Vilcabamba and her farm. I didn't know she seldom went to town, and she only went for short visits. I literally knew nothing of what to expect for the time to come. I was simply in Southern Ecuador, breathing air and being a human.

So, that was yesterday. And that was my first taste of Vilcabamba. Presently, I had just awoken from a nap after that twenty-nine-hour stretch of travel. I was in a bed covered by a sky-blue bug net. Alice had suggested I take a nap at the building on the lower end of the property. I crawled out of bed, got on my feet, and walked outside for a look around.

I was standing on the second-floor, covered-balcony of a supremely rustic, 2600-square-foot house that my friends used as a bed and breakfast. Upstairs, there were three bedrooms. Each had its own bathroom. There was a lounge for guests, furnished with somewhat high-end chairs and couches. Downstairs, there were two his-and-her half baths, a spacious entertaining area, and a full kitchen. I was the only guest and had the place to myself. I was welcomed to pick one of the upstairs rooms as my home for the stay.

This building was striking in its appearance. A blend of cherry-colored stained logs and white stucco construction grabbed my eye. In the rear, the green vertical slope of the mountain seemed to make the house pop confidently from its surroundings. Both floors had brilliant, white tile throughout. The tile extended outside, where it was also used as flooring for the wrap-around balcony where I stood. The handrail was fashioned from tree limbs. Each had been stripped of bark, stained, and sealed. The naturally curvy limbs were cut to fit one another, creating an organic flow. If one aspect of the building lifted the mood the most, it was those remarkable handrails. A brilliant, bright orange terracotta roof topped off the place like a fine hat.

Just looking at the building from a hundred feet away would bring a smile and spark enchantment. From this distance, one could notice how the second floor's dark logs contrasted perfectly with the lower floor's white exterior stucco. Tall, round-topped windows complimented the earthy feel of the building. This place was an incredibly imaginative and inviting getaway. I was floored for being so fortunate to be staying there.

Looking straight out from the front balcony, a lush green and forested Andean ridge ascended some fifteen hundred sheer feet on the other side of the Vilcabamba River. To my left, the river had formed a gap in the mountains where graceful sunrises shed their light on the property. To my right, mountain peaks were layered like scoops of ice cream. They ranged from smallest to largest to the elevated horizon. And all were as green as I was to Ecuador.

Now that I was up and moving, I was simultaneously stimulated by my beautiful surroundings and reined in by the thought, *What now?*

What was there to do for three months? How exactly do you *be* a foreigner? Naturally, I wanted to investigate, take a ton of photos, and share them with my family. All would be happy that I made it alive. So, that was my first move.

I grabbed my video camera and walked to the highest, cleared area of the property. Everything above this point was steep and heavily vegetated mountainside. A small block building was under construction beside me. Once completed, it would house a sensory deprivation tank. From this vantage point, I could see most of the developed property. There were maybe fifty acres cleared. Some had been used for future building lots. Others had been cleared for sugar cane, fruit trees, berry patches, pastures, and flower gardens. This view was not unlike a view of the Garden of Eden.

Straight ahead, a papaya tree boasted a full bunch of nearly ripe papayas. There were bright orange tangerines, mangoes, and lemons of a sweeter variety than tart just down the hill. Below the fruit trees, there was a vegetable garden full of leafy greens ready to complement any salad. To the right, there was a ravine with an avocado tree growing avocados the size of coffee cans! These avocados were larger than the papayas.

I could only glimpse the Vilcabamba River from here, but I could hear it much more so. It was a swift-moving, rocky kayaker's dream. When I spun a circle, the ambiance felt like that of a secret village. Between the robust vegetation, I could spot about a dozen terracotta roofs along the rural road. The stunning mountains entirely surrounded us. A half mile away, the road swept out sight around a sharp curve. Did it lead to another hidden mountain community? I didn't know.

I journeyed down the hill to discover more. My friends had constructed a stone walking path from the top of the property to the door of the B&B. It was several hundred feet long. On either side of the path, the outright quantity of food-growing plant life begged the question: *How can we eat all of this?* I'd come to find that we couldn't.

Alice's home was in this upper area of the property. It was a one-story building with a single-sloped, shallow roof pitch. Much like the B&B, her covered porch had the same striking handrails. The exterior walls were a soft, sand-colored stucco. Inside, the ceiling's height rose to some sixteen feet on one end and sloped to about ten feet on the other. There was a walk-in pantry and a bathroom.

Meanwhile, the rest of the home was a single large room. The tallest wall was nearly all glass and faced the gap in the mountains for a perpetual million-dollar view. They had removed some earth in the rear of the home, giving the structure a feeling of being part of the hillside. Overall, it was a much smaller building than the B&B where I was staying. I came to think of their home as a bungalow. It was absent of cold, sharp angles, and its character seemed pulled from the efficiency and smoothness of nature.

Further down the path, a grove of groomed banana trees played company to two fish ponds stocked with small tilapia. At maturation, they'd add another item to the farm's food menu. Beyond the ponds that sat amongst a dozen more mango trees, a work shed housed all the tools needed to maintain the brilliant level of care given to the land. This was the office, so to speak, for the farm's three full-time caretakers. I had not met the workers at this point. Inside their shed, bananas ripened in a barrel, and machetes waited for trim work. Fuel and lumber were stored alongside coffee-harvesting and processing equipment. Coffee being grown here equaled me being in paradise.

Flowers grew on the farm beyond number. Name a color and there was a flower celebrating it. Ask me what type of flowers they were, and I could give you colorfully perplexed looks just as numerous. These were altogether new species to me—all of them. The stone path then led to two acres of tall grass that fronted the B&B, but this wasn't a yard. It was more like a pasture where I'd learn that a local man would walk two of his enormous bulls there to graze.

The coming days would be full of micro discoveries like the grazing bulls suddenly showing up one morning. There was an afternoon when I chanced upon a flat slug. It had a similar size to the ones I was familiar with on the East Coast of the US, but its body was twice as wide as it was tall. Another morning, I found a little gray bat with a pig-like nose. The farm's squirrels were a collage of orange, black, gray, and white fur. I'd not seen that before. I'm sure there were more than one species of spider; however, I only ever found a species shaped identically to the black and yellow garden spider of my home state.

The evenings further provided discoveries of all sorts. On the first night, I was bit on the foot by a mosquito. For the next two weeks, the spot itched. At home, the itch usually lasted twenty minutes. In the late evenings, I noticed that Ecuador's fireflies blinked in a quick, three-blink pattern, as opposed to North America's single-blink fireflies. And in the sky, I had hoped for the look of millions of shiny pinpoints. After all, we were nowhere near the light pollution of a major city. Though for a reason I cannot understand, the night sky here was shy about sharing the light of its stars.

Without a hint of doubt, I was most surprised by a nighttime discovery during my third night there. It was about 1:30 a.m. I was forced from my sleep by a noise coming from an animal that sounded far too large and far too close. The room I had chosen to live in had a window facing the pasture's less developed side. The forest's edge was just twenty feet away. From somewhere right below my window, a feline moan blasted into my room. A house cat being hot-iron branded couldn't have made a noise that deep. There was, unmistakably, a large cat right outside my window. What's more was that my window happened to be fortified with nothing more than a flimsy, bug screen.

The noise sent a bolt of lightning up my spine. I lay there quietly, just listening. I wondered if it could smell me. *Is it a jaguar?* That was all I could think. Well, that, and: *When is it going to plow through that screen?* The window did have glass shutters should I have had the courage to make a move toward the window to shut them. The last thing I wanted was to head in that direction, or worse, see a jaguar looking up at me. The noise continued four or five more times. I could tell that it was moving back and forth, like trying to figure out how to get through the window. Then it wandered off in a direction that sounded as if it was headed toward the river. I barely slept the rest of the night.

In the morning, I told my friends what I'd heard. They were slow to believe me. They suggested it was just a stray house cat. I wasn't having it. I'd never been scared of any noise from a house cat. The odd thing was the lack of intensity in the cat's sound, yet how deep it was. When ordinary house cats reach their upper threshold of sound, one can easily determine that they are under extreme stress. The animal I heard was far from stressed and would've been frighteningly loud had it been.

With more thought, Alice suggested it may have been a tigrillo. Tigrillos are yellow and black, spotted felines, and are slightly larger than a house cat. I could almost agree with this had it not been for the deep sound. With some research, I found that tigrillos were not known to inhabit that part of Ecuador.

Curiosity urged me to check the jaguar's range. In the past, they did indeed inhabit the entire country. Now, the broadest population is found east of Ecuador's Andes. Further digging uncomfortably confirmed that a few wild jaguars could be found within twenty miles of Vilcabamba at Podocarpus National Park. Given a male jaguar's average home range of up to fifty-three miles, my nightly visitor could've been a jaguar.

The sound was dead on, but the likelihood that it was, was low. Jaguars prefer the dense cloud forests found in the national park. *What else could it be?* Cougars once roamed the area. But it had been a while since their range extended to that part of Ecuador. That left one more possibility—the ocelot. Ocelots are bobcat-sized and native to Ecuador's entirety. They've been weighed at thirty-four pounds which might make them capable of such a deep noise. Though, watching videos of bobcats under extreme stress still didn't confirm the deep feline noise I heard. I may never know just what it was. For the remainder of my stay, the big cat returned like clockwork every two weeks—always making the same uncomfortable noises. I was never brave enough to approach the window for a look.

Each evening, I would supper with my hosts at their bungalow, absorb their Wi-Fi since the B&B didn't have it, and take a long, dark walk down the stone path. I'd walk through the pasture, past the mango groves, and to the B&B to sleep. The ocelot, jaguar, or Ecuadorian forest monster was always at the forefront of my mind. In the daytime, the farm's broad banana leaves, thick flora, and the grove of mango trees supplied the essence of paradise. In the night, they provided the needed hiding place for a jaguar to pounce as I walked by, armed with a flashlight. This dark walk never became comfortable.

Outside of that, and being endlessly hungry, my first week was spent essentially on the farm and in a mountain paradise. It took a few weeks to acclimate to the new diet. My carb-heavy American appetite sent aggressive reminders that I should eat more. Our meals had been of the host's preference. Breakfast was usually an egg scramble laden with vegetables. Lunch might've been soup with a slice of artisan bread and some locally crafted cheese. For dinner, we'd eat a humongous bowl of fruit salad from which each piece was grown on the property. It would be filled with papaya, avocado, mango, bananas, tangerines, blackberries, etc. The diet was fantastically healthy and totally unfamiliar. To swing into McDonald's for a burger and fries just wasn't an option. And, leaving the farm solo to find food to which I was accustomed was not yet an option, either. So, I ate what they provided and hid my hunger.

During the first week, I was unable to escape the farm on my own. We were behind a locked gate. I'd only been to town twice, with Alice, when she needed supplies. There was some apprehension about leaving the new-known on my own. I'd learn there were three ways to leave the farm. I could walk, take a taxi, or ride the bus. The bus schedule was as foreign as this whole experience was to me.

To have transportation of this sort zipping around nameless country roads was even more foreign. For the American mind, try imagining a daily-operated, full-sized passenger bus servicing the farms of rural Kansas, or deep in the mountains of Colorado, or on the winding back roads of Maine. Wouldn't that seem out of place? Yet that's how it was here—intensely rural and highly serviced. Perhaps folks had trouble affording cars. That was likely the reason the bus service existed. I'd never find out if cars were difficult to afford, as I never wanted to push questions upon my host country's citizens regarding their personal finances. It would've been rude. When Alice first mentioned a bus servicing her road, I thought she was crazy. She wasn't. It would pass the farm four times daily.

Taking a taxi was an option of chance. If we made it down the path, across the walk bridge, and up the hill to the road, and a taxi passed by within fifteen minutes, then we were in luck. If one didn't arrive within fifteen minutes, then who knew when the next one would pass? It could be an hour or several hours. Taxi drivers could be called if you had a phone. Between my hosts and me, we had no working phones.

Then there was walking. Just leaving the farm on my own was questionable. I'd have to ask Alice for a key to the locked gate or climb over it. Then, I'd have to walk five miles to Vilcabamba. During these early days, I didn't understand the nature of Ecuadorians enough to stroll along on a path of blind trust and naivety to town. On those two trips to town with Alice, I'd noticed more clearly that the road was accompanied by some nice, and not-so-nice-looking, homesteads. It was not lost on me that I could come up missing if I encountered the wrong individual at the right time.

So, I was kind of stuck at their beautiful property with a tremendous discovery right around the corner. It was more poignant than that of the visit from the nighttime feline. It was category-five homesickness.

I had been in Ecuador for eight days. Somewhat of a pattern had developed regarding a daily routine. We'd have breakfast, lunch, and dinner around the same time. And we would end our evening around the same time. It was about lunchtime when the homesickness kicked in.

We had just finished eating, and I obliged my duties by doing the dishes. Alice was preparing to apply a topical cream to Dan's leg. He was suffering from unnatural swelling and discoloration. Dan was in the restroom. It was a beautiful day. Dish duty was light, and outside the window was a fine view toward the herb garden and a palm-like tree. I was transfixed on the serenity and my fortunate circumstances.

Dan walked behind me, heading for his massage table. Alice was waiting and ready to apply the cream. I'd hardly noticed him in my periphery. The last dish was placed on the drying rack, and I hooked a right toward the kitchen table where my laptop sat opened. Normally, Dan's pant leg would be rolled up to allow Alice access to the affected area—his calf and foot. Today, that method had changed.

While reading something online, my eyes wandered upwardly and focused innocently on their direction. Alice was massaging the cream into his lower leg, and the top of Dan's head was facing me. But something didn't seem right. In only milliseconds, I realized Dan was buck naked from the T-shirt down. I had spotted pubes and skin and nothing more. My eyes fell like lead bricks back to my laptop screen. I could feel a heatwave slide from my heart to my face, powered by an emotional hurricane of thought. *What the hell are they doing?*

Every bit of my decent nature was harassed in that moment. Then, another realization manifested. Dan had left the bathroom and walked right behind me, wearing nothing but a T-shirt. I had heard him climb on the table without first shuffling his pants off. *Why?* was the next thought. *Do they not care that I'm sitting right here facing them?* was the next. And: *What do I do now?* was the thought after that.

All the while, I was freaking the hell out internally while knowing I looked like a radish externally. I knew I had to keep a facial expression of stone. They didn't yet need to know how I felt about their highly odd behavior until I figured out how I would deal with it. In less than thirty seconds, I had gently closed my laptop, stood up calmly, and silently walked out the door. I had to get out of there. Where I'm from, men don't do nude doodle dangling around the house when they have guests over.

Outside on the patio, my mind was in overdrive, and homesickness was quickly settling in. *What do I do? What do I do? What have I gotten myself into? Are these people swingers? Was that a candid way to introduce me to their intentions?* I was panicking. I'll not pretend otherwise. I wanted to be home. I wanted to be a million miles away! *Who the hell are these people?*

When my brain calmed enough to hash out a plan, I reopened my laptop and engaged with airline websites. I wanted to end this trip that second. I checked one site, then another and another. The cheapest flight I could find was $1100. My entire monetary worth was half that. And, with the simplicity of this financial hurdle, my fate was sealed. I was stuck in Ecuador, stuck at their property, and stuck with them for three months.

There was the option of messaging home and begging for the money from my folks or my brother. They would've helped without question. Shame and pride kept my lips sealed in that respect. This wasn't the first time I'd gotten myself in a pickle away from home and needed financial help. The hair-brained idea to come to Ecuador was not looked upon by most as wise. To get rescued by the funds of another would be a true testament to just how stupid I can be. Any wise traveler with two bona fide brain cells wouldn't just up and go to South America for three months with $579. What was I thinking? Only now could I see the naivety in it all. I was forced to revert to the old saying—if you're gonna be dumb, you better be tough.

I'm not sure if Alice and Dan were privy to my leaving the room somewhat abruptly, or just what I was doing outside on my laptop. Although, I knew they could see me through the bungalow's glass wall. I never turned to look inside. Instead, I left for my room and went down the hill, carrying the thickest case of homesickness I'd ever experienced. *What have I gotten myself into?* The question ran on repeat in my mind. What had at first seemed like paradise now felt dark and confined. For the rest of the day, I hid away at the B&B. I was utterly sick over the situation.

In the morning, if I wanted to eat, I knew where I'd have to go. I'd have to go back up the hill and engage with these, now bizarre, strangers. When morning came, it came with hunger. The thought of engaging them was terribly uncomfortable. But it had to be done. The B&B was a food desert at this point. There was fruit growing all around, but my body craved more than that. So, without a solid plan, and a character flaw of being a pushover or sometimes a pathetically nice pushover, I just allowed one foot to follow the other until I reached their door. Confrontation was the last thing I wanted. It's such a turnoff that I'd rather be downwind of a sewer pipe.

I walked in and acted like nothing had ever happened. That's what people like me do. We shove inside of us, even deeper, the thing that's overwhelmingly at the forefront of our thoughts. They did the same, at least on the surface. There seemed an air of just another day in paradise.

I let it ride almost a week before the moment was brought up between Alice and myself. Mental closure was imperative for the trip to Ecuador to not remain regrettable. She had met me at the B&B to talk. As politely as possible, we took a verbal walk around the situation. She explained who Dan was, his experiences, his upbringing, and his comfort level. She gave examples that made sense to me. Though, they were foreign to any experiences I'd had.

She started with Dan being Californian. In a stereotypical sense, she spoke of his nature as laid-back, relaxed, open, secure, and Californian. I'd already deduced this about him. She and I discussed activities he participated in as a young man—free-thinking, hippy activities. We talked about how things had changed in regard to nudity and conservatism between the sixties and now. For instance, he grew up showering openly after gym class. I did not. It wasn't something we did in West Virginia in the nineties. We just went to the next class sweaty. To Dan, nudity was no big deal. To me, nudity is saved for dating.

Both Alice and Dan portrayed unwavering comfort in their own skin. It was me who may have needed to loosen up. I could stand to make a few strides toward being a more open person. I'm not saying that I needed to become a nudist or even become comfortable with their extreme openness. Though, part of the reason for coming to Ecuador was growth. It was already manifesting.

To expand this growth further, I'd have to figure out how to get around in Ecuador on my own. First, I started with getting to town and back. It was the end of the second week there, and the bus would soon be on its way. I asked Alice to unlock the gate. I went down the hill, across the swinging bridge, and to the end of the trail.

Across the road was an old, block homestead typical for the area. It was worn, gray, and unpainted, somewhat do-it-yourself in nature. It played the role of a leaning post and bus stop for the locals. Some folks were standing there. I approached with an "Hola." I received that in return, as well as more Spanish words than I could understand. I think they were trying to figure out who I was and where I was from. So, I replied with, "El Estados Unidos." (The United States) I had that much figured out. They wanted to know if I was staying with Alice and for how long. My Spanish was wretched at this point, but I caught the vibe of the questions. I answered the best I could.

The bus rounded a sharp corner. A few hands were lofted to hail it. We boarded. I paid the sum of twenty-five cents; American. The trip was only five miles but felt like an adventure. People looked at me. I looked back, looking for the one who might give me trouble. No one did.

The bus weaved back and forth in the green mountain curves. I paid extreme attention to my surroundings, noting possible landmarks. These would be vital, should I miss the bus, have to walk back, or direct a taxi driver back. It's a weird thing to be on edge and mystified at the same time. The landscape had me crushing on it the way a young man might nervously engage his female interest. I wanted to be on the way to town. I wanted to be among these mountains. I wanted to feel a culture different than mine, but all safe enough to return to West Virginia with stories.

In Vilcabamba, the bus stopped, and I stepped off. Alice had told me about a place called Timothy's. She said they had great burgers there. Given the perfectly healthy diet I'd been eating, I was ready for a burger—and a beer.

Timothy's was a couple blocks over from the bus stop. A feeling came over me walking toward it. Now, I'm finally *being* a foreigner. I'm figuring out the lay of the land and getting around on my own. Being stuck behind the locked gate at the farm, while in the company of two English speakers, had yet to provide the experience of truly feeling foreign. The first days had felt similar to a vacation, but now as I walked Vilcabamba alone, a reactivated state of heightened alertness took the fun out of being out and about.

That paranoia comes from me not being the type of person to expect everyone around me to instantly like me or welcome me. It's a character flaw developed in my youth school experiences. More than being sought for friendship, I experienced life as being sought for the subject of jokes, over being poor and red-headed. I've learned that anything can happen at any time and with anyone—no matter my heart or intentions. My modus operandi is it's best to be aware.

I experienced no trouble making it to Timothy's. Surprisingly, it was everything you'd expect of a dive bar in the States. Memorabilia plastered the walls in such color and quantity that the eye was forcibly busy. I was okay with the place feeling slightly of home. I was still easing my way into this new country. I ordered a burger, fries, and a beer. I took a seat on their outside patio and opened my notepad. It was time to capture what these first days had been like while they were still fresh. And, by God, the first couple bites of that burger were an unbelievably welcomed change over the lean cuisine on which I'd been chewing.

As I sat there, folks strolled by Timothy's in an unamazed fashion. If they were locals, they acted like it. If they were out-of-towners, they had a backpack on and looked like they were looking for their accommodations. No one looked anxious. In what was more unexpected than usual, having the beer eased the tension in my shoulders so much that I could breathe freer than in weeks. I could smile and relax as I turned everything that had happened into notes. I could look around and appreciate the construction styles found here. I could appreciate that I was in a foreign country. It was the first time I truly felt comfortable being in Ecuador. I was finally here and happy to be.

A Family Christmas

When I was a boy, Christmas had all the magic for which a child could hope. Family came from faraway lands, like the other side of the county, or the next state over, to unite as one unit. To me, some were heroes, while others were friends, aunts, uncles, and cousins. Of course, far away back then felt much further away than it does now. Growing up and learning to drive tends to shrink the world.

Back then, we'd gather at grandma's house. She was the glue that held the tribe together. She was the reason for the season. Her sons and daughters would gather up their little ones, bringing them along for a jolly communion in her tight and cozy house. The limited space made the feeling even more personal. It was just what was needed to squeeze the most out of the one day a year that I was guaranteed to get to see some of my favorites. Gifts and playtime were all that mattered then. The tradition went on and we got older.

Then, in 2006, the tradition stopped. I was twenty-five years old. The glue needed for the season went away. Our family lost our mother, grandmother, and to some, our great grandmother. Being in my twenties, I suppose I was not yet learned enough to predict the end of those magical Christmases. When Christmas came the following year, it was much quieter. And they've been that way since—until Ecuador.

Two weeks before the holiday, we got an invitation to celebrate Christmas with Iliana, Alice's doctor. Her office was over in Loja. Alice, Dan, and I went to Iliana's for a scheduled treatment on Dan's leg. Iliana had worked on his condition for a while. She had advised him to wear a specialized compression sock and keep his leg elevated.

Seeing Iliana for the first time, while in her working capacity, birthed a grin I was forced to suppress. She came in wearing a skirt, and she was highly attractive. Given some sort of shallow perspective I'd yet to mature past, it was hard to see her as a doctor. I found it impossible to ignore her attire and general good looks. Her makeup was on point. Her hair was fixed perfectly for giving off signals to a signal-picker-upper like myself that she knew she was attractive. The fact that I couldn't understand anything she was saying made her even more intriguing.

Now, on Christmas Eve, it was a pleasure to board the bus and ride an hour and a half through the striking scenery to Loja. The paved road there mimicked a technique used in trail building that I'd noticed on portions of the Appalachian Trail. To conquer the sheer slopes of the Andes, these roads were designed in a continual zig-zag. Back and forth, the roads wandered perpendicular to the rise of the mountains. There were miles of only slight elevation gains. We'd go a mile in one direction, but then, we'd take a 170-degree turn and travel a mile going in the opposite direction. We'd come to a hairpin turn and then slowly climb toward another hairpin. For those who get nauseous easily, and I did, the zig-zags were a challenge. They were amplified by the hard acceleration and deceleration of a bus driver attempting to remain on time. Thankfully, the scenery removed most of my mind's focus enough to somewhat fight off nausea.

Once in Loja, we arrived at the bus terminal that scared me to my wits end a couple weeks before. Iliana's office was about a mile away. We decided to walk. I took great pleasure in noticing the novelties of the city of Loja. Here, there were concrete telephone poles. They were sometimes round and sometimes square. Often, they had structural holes designed into them. The cars, passing by, were of smaller models than in the States. They were new and clean. Altogether, nothing seemed odd with them. They just seemed a bit under-powered. I wondered if they were three-cylinder models. Folks were dressed really nicely and walking around with smartphones. This shouldn't have been a surprise. But I was still rather green to being in a foreign country.

Illiana's office matched a theme I noticed in Vilcabamba. It was behind a locked gate—a tall, very sturdy locked gate. My mind couldn't help but wonder about the reason to fortify in this way. I wondered, *Is Loja riddled with crime, or are the police lousy here?* In the States, a fortified entrance might mean you're entering a government facility, an upper-class neighborhood, or a ranch full of livestock looking for ways out. But these examples are hard for me to conjure, given the mostly sparse usage of walls and heavy gates in the US. Fences in the US are a different story.

Iliana's gate was unlocked. Once inside, a buzzer system allowed her to know it was us. She remotely unlocked the door. This time, we went further than the doctor's office. We went upstairs to her home. I was surprised by this. It was the third and top floor of the building. Inside, a contemporary layout felt condo-like. Vaulted ceilings and a light-colored paint scheme gave the place an air of being larger than it was. In one corner of the living room, a nativity scene represented the holiday season.

We were welcomed in a supremely hospitable fashion by Iliana and her husband Carlos. I felt like a friend in less than five minutes. I'd briefly met Carlos at one of Dan's previous doctor appointments. Carlos had been working with Iliana in what seemed like a role of doctor's assistant, though I was unable to verify this. Nor did I understand his relationship with her then. Now, inside his home, I realized he and Iliana were married. A brief look around showed me that he worked in the doctor's office, but his heart belonged to music. He was a professional musician with an entire room dedicated to his instruments.

Within a half hour, Alice was in conversation with Iliana in Spanish. Dan was taking care of some things online. I'd gotten to that point where my awkward bone, the size of West Virginia's Eastern Panhandle, was beginning to show. I could no longer keep up with the conversation and was stuck feeling mildly out of place. You can only make eye contact and smile so many times before the inner voice says, *You're crazy. Don't even pretend.* I got a hint from Alice that I could go outside to the deck and then to the roof of Iliana's house to stretch my legs.

In the middle of the porch, a huge stem of bananas was hanging to ripen, and clothes were drying on a clothesline. I personally loved seeing this. Growing up, we hung clothes out to dry. Mom often directed me to wrangle them off the line. Alice and Dan also hung their clothes on a line at their bungalow. Still, I had not given that much thought. Being Americans from an earlier generation, somewhat frugal, and advocates for the environment, I knew their angle. When I saw this at Iliana's, it really sunk in that this was still commonplace in Ecuador.

I was in tune with this welcomed, extra degree of simplicity. People from modest, rural backgrounds don't need convenience at their fingertips. They're hardier. Urban life makes you soft and can kind of drive you nuts with all the choices to be made and gadgets to be had. Clothes dryers are one of those. They're expensive both in retail price and electricity usage. A look around Loja showed me nearly everyone was hanging their clothes.

It's so practical, and somehow, we've largely moved past that in the States. In reflection, we moved past it so deftly that I can't remember the moment where we didn't do it anymore. The trade-off for a dryer's convenience is just one more thing that keeps us inside closer to the TV and closer to the snacks and couch.

I left the deck for the roof of Iliana's home. I opened a door to a flat, concrete roof without a railing. Looking out from here, the view was noticeably similar to urban Southern California. Though, maybe greener. Loja was a city of 150,000. The sprawl of Los Angeles wasn't matched in this background, but homes were built on hillsides in much the same way you'd see in the Hollywood Hills. The thought of that style of development was running through my mind so fully, I bet I'd blurt out "SoCal" if you stuck me on Iliana's roof and gave me a one-second chance to gaze at my surroundings and answer where I was. What was odd was that I had already had this strange sense while walking the streets of Vilcabamba. *Gosh, Ecuador's terrain feels like California.*

A significant difference in staring out at Southern California, and staring out at Loja, was the rainbow of small, colorful homes dotting the hillsides and their terracotta roofs. Perhaps nowhere in the States exists a city full of such colorfully painted homes and businesses. I was a little lifted in mood at this realization. Feeling rather comfortable, I whipped out my camera, walked the perimeter of the roof, and began narrating a video to share with my family. I was smiling, pointing, and enjoying the eighty-degree temperature. Sunshine was plentiful. Things looked beautiful.

Down below, a street was moderately filled with cars. In an orange car of some unfamiliar make, a fella riding passenger noticed me on the roof. He hung torso-deep out the window and screamed at me. He was looking dead at me. His arm lofted to full extension and the cherry on top was that finger between the pointer and the ring. I was dumbfounded.

Moments before, I was in total appreciation for this foreign city. Now, an internal current ran deep within of feeling unwelcome. What he yelled, I have no idea. In an instant, the thought, *I really need to watch my back here,* bubbled to the surface. Everything that I had experienced to help me begin to feel comfortable in Ecuador slipped right through my fingers. *Did this man express what they really think of foreigners? If I walked these streets alone, would I be attacked?*

Assuredly, this man couldn't meet a foreigner much nicer than myself with zero intention to bring negativity to his homeland. Even knowing this of myself, the interaction left me internally down for quite a while. Externally, I suppressed it. I was aware that I had just experienced being on the receiving end of a verbal hazing like the ones spouted in my country by citizens who express hatred toward foreigners and minorities. It's a heavy feeling. It's a feeling that could make the world a better place if everyone had the opportunity to face the humility born from it. Instead, most never leave their comfort zones. I went back inside. We'd soon leave for Iliana's father's house in another part of Loja.

Every practical part of me knew that I was in great company with Iliana and her family. Still, the quick encounter with the irate man had me secretly hoping everyone would welcome Alice, Dan, and myself along for Christmas.

Bolivar, Iliana's father, was the glue holding the family together. Just like my grandmother was, he was the central character for this Christmas. Relatives from all around came to see him and to spend time with family. He was a man of pristine Spanish dictation matched with patience, sincerity, and listening. The way he so clearly and concisely pronounced his words made it easier for me to understand them. In our brief interactions, I suspect he was aware that I was listening and attempting to comprehend to my best ability. I already admired this man for the role he had and how undeniably devoted his family was to him. Eighteen folks were the count, including myself, that were happy to be together accompanying him.

His home had a small kitchen and spacious living room. The large gathering made things a bit tight in the kitchen. I took a seat for the first hour at a table in the living room where a woman and her two children sat. Alice used her perfect Spanish to mingle. Dan mainly stayed by her side. At the table, a very young girl dared to interact with me. Realizing there was no number of words we'd be able to exchange, I offered her my sunglasses. She put them on, and I snapped photos of her. Then, I spun around the camera so she could see them. I was fine with starting small and getting to know everyone since I was the odd man out.

As the night wore on, internal tensions wore off inside me. As best I could, I tried to keep up. I continued to use my camera as an icebreaker and made an offering of family photos to be shared afterward. The night became an incredibly wholesome time, just like the ones I had missed. The family was brilliant—funny, welcoming, and genuinely appreciative of their foreign visitors. I even managed to enjoy a couple healthy laughs.

One came when I spotted the turkey through the oven door window. Someone had arranged its neck between its legs in such a way that it looked like a penis pointing northward. Though I couldn't grasp the lingo regarding this, there was no mistaking the pointing, gesturing, and giggles associated with the contorted bird. We found that Carlos, and Iliana's brother, who was also named Bolivar, were responsible for the turkey's condition. They reminded me of one of my uncles and one of my crazy cousins—the practical jokers of the family.

There was another moment where someone funneled my attention toward an attractive female family member. She had come all the way from Ecuador's eastern coast to visit. She was highly pleasing to the eyes, and I'd noticed her milliseconds after arriving. As a writer, I have words galore if needed. But as a foreigner who would've loved to talk to her, having access to a million English words was the equivalent to having duct tape over my mouth. My slim grin was the only tool of communication I had. Trying to talk to her went nowhere.

Still, it wasn't all about that. It was all about a family being happily together as a large, loving unit. Christmas Eve concluded with a family portrait. I set my Canon camera on a timer. We took ten rapid snapshots, each one getting a little sillier. The final shot was full of wild ear-to-ear grins and hands in the air. I couldn't have asked for more.

But there was so much more. That was just the beginning of their Christmas celebration. Every bit of enjoyment I got from that evening was enough to leave me smiling. Yet, it was great to learn we'd all be spending the next day together and have even more of a gathering. I was learning this on the fly. Alice tried to fill me in, but until each new aspect of their holiday celebration surfaced, I didn't have a clue as to what would really happen.

We awoke at Iliana's place. She prepared a breakfast of hard-boiled eggs, some fruit, and a pastry to which I was foreign. An easygoing morning passed, and we left to join Iliana's family at their shared homestead in another part of Loja.

We arrived at a home of incredibly basic construction. Behind another locked gate and block wall were a few structures resembling habitable but highly weathered farm buildings. Some were like closed-in lean-tos. A section of the main structure looked like it once served as bedrooms. It was painted a wine-colored red with white-trimmed, single-pane windows. In its entirety, the largest building may have been thirty feet long with six-and-a-half-foot ceilings. I had to duck through the doorways. I gathered that this place may have been a childhood home for the eldest of the family. Or, it may have been the home of a family member a generation, or two, older than that person. I got the impression that it hadn't always sat closed in by a wall and locked gate. My imagination could see these structures sitting alone in a field long before the neighboring buildings were erected.

Passing through the gate and stepping down four or five wide steps from the street, a two-story building's painted white brick wall was on your right. The main structure was straight ahead, constructed into an Lshape toward the left. Immediately to the left, a separate building of more primitive construction seemed to be used as storage. In all, these features enclosed a tiny courtyard of half concrete slab and half grassy yard. It made for a courtyard about fifteen by twenty feet.

Southern Ecuador's weather was often so perfect that a need for heating and air conditioning really hadn't arisen. That set of structures were fingerprints to a time where people may have lived without doors or windows. Although there were both doors and windows installed, they were probably added at a later point. I still mentally kick myself sometimes for not finding out more about the history of their family home.

It intrigued me in the sense that a family home could be like the glue needed after losing someone who had held the family together. At one of my former jobs, there was an employee whose family owned an estate where they'd gather for the holidays. Once I knew this, I was instantly sold on the idea. I thought something like that might bring my family back together. Here in Ecuador, the family home had worked as a perfectly shared gathering hub.

Upon entering the homestead, the story was pretty clear. Iliana's family didn't use this place all the time. It was just occupied on the holidays. Plants were overgrown. Things were covered and stowed away. Some of the women began to clean the kitchen and set out tables. A couple of the men started cleaning a mess of mud and water that was inches deep and clogging a drain on the concrete slab. I watched for a minute, unsure of what to do. Then I thought: *Hey, I'm just a hillbilly from West Virginia. Let me give these boys a hand.*

We were scooping out mud by the bare handful; no shovels. It smelled horrible! It had been a half hour there, and I was comfortably filthy up to the elbow. The last thing I wanted to portray was being a first-world, goody-two-shoes that was afraid of getting his hands dirty; a pretty boy. These fine folks were planning to feed us later, after all. Helping was the least I could do.

Later, a large, long-haired man arrived with a guitar and a set of speakers on tripods. There was a table in front of him that was filling with stuff to snack on. Carlos dawned a ridiculous-looking, pink cooking apron as he manned the grill. These guys were all about a good fire. I saw them using a blow dryer to intensify the flame. This was definitely reminiscent of hillbilly ingenuity. I loved it, and if I'd a thought they would've caught on, I would've shared a solid, "Yeehaw!"

Around us, people were filing in. The place was looking cleaner, and things were shaping up for a celebration. The music man began to play. I imagined his songs were traditional folk songs. Some could have been love songs. Most had that happy, upbeat tempo found in Latin American music. Of course, this is a non-translated guess. They all could have been Christmas songs. There was no way for me to tell.

While looking around, there were smiling faces, children, old-timers, and a couple stray cats playing despite their usually quiet home being taken over. Slowly, in the transition from an unused homestead to a holiday gathering place, I began to see the appeal of the old buildings. The setting was intimate. There was no doubt a few hearts were dearly connected to the place.

The day slid on. I couldn't have wanted to be anywhere else. Surprises came in each moment. One was a hot drink made of milk and dark brown cane sugar. A large pot-full became popular once it was ready. It was incredibly sweet—like warm ice cream. The amount of sugar used could have fed a hundred hummingbirds for life. It was the first I'd seen this drink. It certainly tasted fantastic, but it wouldn't be something to have every day. However, in the US, many of us ingest sugar in similar quantities through sodas and snack cakes. I kept the servings to just two.

An unforeseen surprise came from Iliana's brother, Bolivar, and his three children; Pablo, Ariel, and Maria. His children knew enough English that, when combined with my slowly gained Spanish, we could converse as smoothly as driving a pothole-laden street. It was possible to keep moving forward enough to get to where we were going.

His sons were avid motocross fans. This was the surprise. Motocross dominated my life as a teen and twenties-something. These young men displayed the same sort of passion in their eyes and enthusiasm in their voices that I felt at their age. You know it's your favorite thing when you catch yourself smiling wildly in moments of conversation. The young men knew of places to ride all over the US without ever having been there. Some of their favorite racers were my favorite racers. Their father was just as in tune.

I told them of how I was a fan of Ecuador's most famous racer: Martin Davalos. Martin was one of the world's greats. By then, he'd been a factory-sponsored, elite motocross racer for a decade. In the States, I had the chance to see him race a dozen times. This connection through sport solidified these guys as instant life-long friends.

Could Christmas with this family get any better? Well, it depends if you enjoy dancing. If you do not, this is where culture shock would get the best of you. If you do, this is where you get to take center stage and let some soul out. I happened to enjoy dancing—while drinking. So, it was with mixed emotion, as a night of perfect temperature fell upon us, that I was forced to dance for nearly two hours.

The old muddy concrete slab was now dry from the Christmas Day sun. This became our dance floor. Folks were shaking a leg for the past half hour. The music man had gone strong for some six or seven hours without signs of letting up. I was in my head deeply at this point, thinking, *Look at this! We have a celebration on our hands now! I sure hope they don't ask me to dance.* With a half-gallon of whiskey and a familiar beat, I'm game. Being dry of drink and a newborn to this genre of tunes, I wanted no part of it beyond witnessing it. This was where I wished my command of the Spanish word for 'No,' which is 'No,' would've been more powerful. I tried and tried, but my resistance was ignored. With no way out, I was to dance and dance my little heart out.

I set my camera to record toward the dance floor. I made my move—elbows and ankles at the ready. Being a white guy, I was about to show these Ecuadorians what a butter knife would look like dancing if it had knee joints. I was second in a line of five people, who were dancing three feet from another line of five. The dancers were facing each other. It wasn't a couple's dance. It was rhythmic individual gyration.

Iliana's sister was right across from me. I didn't know whether to look at her or look around. I didn't know if she was single or married. She was doing something like a fast Texas two-step with more hips. I was doing something reminiscent of a person mid-trip and about to fall. Two dancers down from me, a ninety-four-year-old man had a perfectly timed shuffle going on. One of Iliana's cousins was a man in flip flops who had found an extra beat to move to in between the beats I was barely keeping up with. He'd match that with a celebratory cheer and high-knee moves and lofted arms. He was the showcase dancer of the group. I was like, "That's how you do it, man!"

On we danced! Another long hour passed—marathoning it. During a brief pause in the music, I spotted a nearby brick ledge to sit on. My forehead and armpits were leaking with sweat. It felt good. I was happy to have obliged their request for me to dance. A young gal even came over to give me something refreshing to drink. I grabbed the tiny cup, thinking I could drink four cups of water that size. I nearly spit it out when I found that every last bit of it was filled with warm wine! Oh my! I wasn't ready for it. I thanked her and tried asking for some water. Just then, Iliana came over and grabbed my arm. It was time for me to start dancing again.

The only option for getting out of it would've been saying, "No! No! No!" and meaning it. Although I thought that could've come across as rude so, I didn't resist. Certainly, saying, "Iliana. Please. I'm tired, and it cannot possibly be of any benefit for me to continue these seizure-like movements in front of all these innocent people," was not an option. No, sir. No, ma'am. Saying that in English or attempting to in Spanish would've, again, got me nowhere. On we danced, for another hour—solid.

Last evening, on Christmas Eve, I was able to relive the magic of the holidays not felt in a decade. On this ordinary Christmas Day in Loja, Ecuador, I shared in the love and spirit and energy that lived eternally in the walls of that old homestead. The Christmas with Iliana's family revealed all the magic I could have hoped for and so much more.

Mamita Building and Macas

The morning after Christmas, we said our thank yous and goodbyes to Iliana. Carlos gave us a ride to Loja's bus terminal. Alice and Dan were heading back to beautiful Vilcabamba, while I was bussing twelve hours northeast to Macas, Ecuador—the capital of the Morona Santiago Province. Oddly, I already had a friend there. Going to see her would remove me from the magnificence of the steep Andes. I'd move into the land at the very western edge of the Amazon jungle. I was heading straight for total immersion into Ecuadorian culture.

For the next two weeks, it was possible that I'd not hear a spec of English come out of another human's mouth. The point of all this was to visit a wonderful woman in both vitality and spirit named Lucia. I met Lucia in October 2016 at Alice's house in West Virginia. This was the same house I worked on to earn my stay in Ecuador. She had come to the States to spend a couple weeks as Alice's guest.

It wasn't her first time in America. Lucia had a handful of prior vacations in the US. But her loyalties laid where her heart certainly lived—in her beloved Ecuador. Speaking English was never much of a necessity to her. On days that I'd come over to work on Alice's house, Lucia and I would exchange smiles and the most basic of greetings. I might have said, "¿Cómo estás?" (How are you) And I could only reply with, "Bien." (Good) But if I asked her, "¿Cómo estás?" and her reply went further than "Bien," I'd be lost.

    Lucia left an impression on me of her entire country during her couple of weeks in West Virginia. I noticed her tremendous humility, her soft-spoken nature, and her endless stream of smiles. I genuinely wished I could converse with her. I would've liked to have found out what she thought of West Virginia and know if there was anything she'd like to do while visiting. However, I did know for sure that she was freezing her innocent little butt off. In upper-forty to lower sixty-degree weather, which I'd call nearly perfect for October, she was often huddled next to Alice's woodstove. I'd soon find out why the cold affected her when I made it to Ecuador.

    During Lucia's stay in West Virginia, there was an evening when I decided to work late at Alice's. With that decision, Alice allowed me to stay over instead of driving home. I fashioned a bed out of piled blankets downstairs beside the wood stove. Most of the lights in the house were off. Lucia came downstairs and sat beside me. She wanted to show me pictures of Ecuador on her phone. I could also sense her wanting to chat. We tried until our wits end to speak to each other.

Though, there was little success. We settled with exchanged smiles as she scrolled through her photos. Now in Ecuador, and on the way to see her again, I was hoping the language barrier wouldn't ruin my visit.

From Loja's bus terminal to Macas, I'd get my first real taste of Ecuador outside of the Andes. The route was largely two-lane pavement over countless bridges and ravines with fast-rushing water below. We'd pass through towns with highly exotic names like Zamora, Yantzaza, Bomboiza, and Gualaquiza. These were towns with tremendous swaths of forest in between. We passed peaks in the mountains so incredibly green and spired that I'd nearly lose my breath in gaze.

One peak soared God-like into the clouds. Every summit around it fell short of making it to the clouds. I wasn't sure as to why it rose so high. I simply, rather desperately, wanted the clouds to clear before the bus lurched out of sight. Did that peak begin to round off above the cloud line, or did it soar another 2,000 feet? I didn't know. Multiple attempts to search online for that location revealed nothing.

In Gualaquiza, I had to acquire another ticket to transfer bus services. I was on the bus some six hours by then, having to pee for the last four. There were two stops before Gualaquiza. One was brief, and one was a half hour. During those stops, I decided to stay seated on the bus instead of pee. For the life of me, I could not tell when the bus would leave. Without Alice to translate, I was a sitting duck. Where the bus went, I went. Do not leave the bus. Do not let the bus leave me. That was my survival tactic.

From Gualaquiza to Macas, the land took on a

different look. This is a far stretch of the imagination, but it looked like what I imagine Thailand to look like. I noticed how an odd palm would jut out from the undergrowth to a soaring height. And the mountains weren't as peaked here. It also seemed that the temperature was warmer than I'd felt since arriving in Ecuador. The bus rolled on through this new landscape.

At one stop, we picked up three children. One of them sat with me. His name was Domingo. This kid had the widest and whitest smile possible on a human his size. He was a curious sort. He chose to sit with the strange-looking foreigner rather than take one of the open seats elsewhere. We began instantly talking. He didn't seem to mind Spanglish or that I had little comprehension of his words. He just kept talking. His words were probably questions. Who knows? He rode the bus with me for ten miles and then departed. Soon after, darkness began to fall.

The arrival of nighttime spawned a sense within me that I'd missed my stop. I was traveling without a phone or a map. All hope rested on seeing something that said Macas on it. About three towns, and an hour before Macas, it was pitch black. I didn't have a clue if I'd missed my stop or not. I just held out hope that it would still only take twelve hours. And we weren't at twelve hours yet.

When the bus arrived in Macas, it was about 8:30 p.m. The terminal was larger than most stops we'd encountered. When we pulled up, I spotted Lucia standing outside. Seeing her felt incredibly similar to seeing Alice for the first time in Vilcabamba. The sight of Lucia meant I wasn't lost, that I hadn't ridden the bus too far, and that I could relax. I grabbed my bags and unloaded.

As I looked around, the bus terminal was energetic with people. Lucia approached and greeted me with a smile pulled from her bucketful of smiles. Accompanying her was a teenaged girl named Josie. The three of us took off into the night, away from the bus terminal. I was completely unsure as to where we were headed and expected to go to Lucia's house.

Macas was well-lit. The buildings were of similar construction as observed in other parts of Ecuador. I was able to decipher quite soon that we weren't headed to Lucia's home. Rather, we were to explore Macas and its Christmas decorations. Lucia wanted to show me her dear city right away.

We wandered in a large loop through streets speckled with Christmas spirit. There was a town square with a jumbo-sized Christmas tree, a makeshift train decorated as finely as Santa's sleigh, and a large display of illuminated, primary-colored letters spelling Macas. It was an immediate photo opp. Like Vilcabamba, the center of Macas was defined by its church. A tall and wide staircase below its entry seemed to exaggerate the church's size. There was a divine feeling being at its doorstep in the night, in this town, so mysterious to me.

We walked for a half hour then arrived at Lucia's home. She lived at the far end of a narrow alley made of thin, three-story attached homes. Most of the bottom floors were being used commercially, including Lucia's home. We arrived at a house full of people. This immediate immersion came far faster than I had expected. Given my Christmas in Loja, this shouldn't have come as a surprise. In the same breath that I say that, few hang around after Christmas Day in the United States. It's back-to-work time and back to the grind. Culturally, it would just be weird. I assumed everyone was still there for the holidays—extended.

Lucia's mother, Maria, her sisters, Blanca and Linda, and her brother, Angel greeted me with smiles and Spanish. They were overwhelmingly welcoming. I appreciated the smiles. Everyone quickly discovered that my command of Spanish needed a lot of work. I was tested a couple times to see where my level of tongue was. This led to laughter among them and confusion on my part. Though, Angel made sure that I knew I was welcomed. He put two English words together and said, "No bully." He wanted me to know they were just playing around.

Lucia provided her bedroom for my stay. It was on the third level of her home and interestingly detached from the rest of the home. If you were to enter her house from the street, you'd notice Lucia's naturopathic clinic on the lowest floor. Beside that entrance, a door led to a staircase to the second floor. Here was the home's kitchen, bathroom, and living room. To reach the third floor, you'd take a centralized and tiled staircase just off the kitchen.

I loved the layout of the third floor. It was completely exposed to the elements, with only two sides of it having walls. One was the wall that joined the adjacent home. The other was a wall belonging to Lucia's bedroom. Overhead, there was a tin roof supported by metal framing. The bedroom, an open-air laundry area, and a small flower garden finished off the third floor. What was so interesting was how the equatorial weather allowed homeowners to live in a home completely exposed to the elements. Sure, rain couldn't make it in, thanks to the roof; but wind, humidity, temperature, and insects could. Walking up the stairs to the third floor, nothing was separating the outside from the inside. It sparked the imagination and felt treehouse-like.

I thought, I would love to have this feature on a house in West Virginia. Of course, if winters weren't so cold, and summers so hot, and mosquitoes so plentiful, and if building codes weren't so strict. And so on, and so on. If there was a flaw in the design, it's that it was a bit warm to sleep up there. For Lucia, that was a non-issue. She thrived in Macas's slightly warmer climate. I preferred to sleep in much lower temperatures. We called it a night after several wholesome hours with the family.

It took me a while to fall asleep. In the blackness of night, I heard a knock at the door. It seemed to come only moments after dozing off. Though, it was 4:30 a.m. Lucia called my name in a drawn-out fashion that I'd come to recognize as her way of saying it. She would say, "Miiike." Her version of my name sounded as if she'd added a couple long 'I's. I wondered what in the world was going on. Was there an emergency? I responded with an "Hola." She opened the door and said something. All I could grasp through the grogginess was that I needed to come with her. I picked up on the word taxi since it's the same in both languages. Trustfully, I followed her downstairs. I climbed into a taxi with her, Blanca, and Josie. We drove away, and I was barely awake.

Where we were going was beyond my comprehension so completely that my imagination briefly entertained I'd been kidnapped. Were we headed to a remote homestead where my organs were going to be harvested? Sure, that thought actually came to mind, as thoughts do. Though, I didn't give it much credibility.

The taxi left Macas behind for a dirt road with tall plants bordering each side. The headlights provided an eerie vibe. I'd be lying if I didn't admit that I was on guard again upon reaching the dirt road. Inside the cab, the girls were laughing and joking about things I'll never understand. In their chatter, the words "mamita building" kept popping up. I took this as a clue as to where we were headed. But what in the world was a mamita building?

The taxi driver crept a couple miles up that dirt road and released us in a parking area high on a ridge. We set off on foot. The chatter, "mamita building," gained in frequency. It was still pitch black. But now, it was just the girls and me. I was losing the worried edge. In a life or death situation, I could surely outrun them. The road took on a bend. As we rounded the last of it, I found out what this was all bout. There, I laid eyes upon a giant statue of a woman—Mamita Building!

There was an eighty-foot-tall statue of a robed woman elevated upon a four-story-tall structure. Soft, blue light illuminated her majesty. She was a sight! Lucia had planned this right under my nose without me knowing. She wanted to show me one of the treasures belonging to her beloved Macas.

We climbed a spiral staircase to a viewing platform

at the feet of the statue. Below, the entirety of Macas laid before us. Hundreds of yellow and white lights glowed like stars speckling the small city. Further out, I could see moonlight shimmering off the Upano River and black forest surrounding it. Macas's central cathedral still seemed prominent from this distance. Turning around to have a look, Mamita Building's toes were as long as my legs. She was holding her palms together, in a praying formation, with her head compassionately tilted forward. I was so happy to be with the girls in this moment overlooking Macas. What a surprise! I gathered that Lucia had wanted to catch the sunrise from here. It was the perfect place.

During the hour on the platform, I tried to make sense of why it was called Mamita Building. Together, Josie's and Blanca's English was just enough to enlighten me on my mistake. When it hit me that they had been saying Mamita Virgin all along, I belly laughed. To my English ear, hearing those native Spanish speakers saying virgin sounded like beerheen. My simple brain had morphed beerheen into building. Spanish V's sound like English B's, while their G's sound like our H's. Clueless, I was.

The sun rose. It revealed thickly forested, rolling hills which ran in all directions surrounding Macas. They weren't high Andes. These were more like foothills. The high mountains were nowhere in sight. The river looked a couple miles off. It hosted a bridge, going who knows where into the unbroken forest. A growing curiosity spurred a moment of inspired Spanish. When I asked her, Lucia confirmed that this region was part of the Amazon Jungle. It was high-elevation jungle, reaching 3000-plus feet.

We left Mamita Virgin for a hike down the dirt road back to Macas. It was a beautiful, blue-skied Eastern Ecuadorian day. Lucia used her trained eye for medicinal plants to pluck some herbs. Likewise, she took the time to show me her native flora. She'd spot an orchid and glow with delight. She'd say, "¡Miiike, mira!" (Mike, look!) Or she'd spot a mimosa plant and tap it with her hands. We'd watch as the leaves would instantly fold in upon themselves. Novelty was rich in the moment. I'd never seen a plant instantly react to anything other than fire. We became serial mimosa flickers as we strolled along.

This morning was the beginning of two weeks of dense novelty saturation. I was happy to be there. Later that day, I was on the third floor of Lucia's house writing notes when I looked out onto the horizon. On the nearest ridge outside of town, I spotted Mamita Virgin. She looked tiny from there.

Genuine Ecuador

Claiming to know the reality of a place is tough without direct experience. I think you can understand what's real by going and feeling, meeting, and reflecting. Regarding culture, you must interact with its people. Finding what's real can't quite be done remotely. News outlets are patently incapable of showing you the real side of a place to which you've never been. Their selling you on a location's pros and cons is only wasted breath. Often, their focus lies heavily on the cons. In real life, that intensity is rarer than advertised. I have come to know this as truth through my travels. Ultimately, what we experience and conclude is subjective.

    I surely wasn't forced to travel to Macas. Instead, I went to visit Lucia in hopes of experiencing a genuine existence as Ecuadorians lived it. Unlike Vilcabamba, Macas was nearly void of foreigners. It was a city without a single hint of a tourism economy. My time there showed me that my friends, and their town, were armed to the teeth with unique, natural, and societal subtleties just waiting for a set of foreign eyes.

Awkwardness owned the situation during one of the first of these noticed subtleties. Lucia's mother, Maria, served me a soup that I couldn't bring myself to eat. The soup was of a broth and vegetable mix. Lurking in the deepest part of the bowl was something that resembled a tiny, mutated alien's spine. I snagged it with my fork and brought it to the surface. Once exposed, I wasn't sure what to do with it. The first thought I had while it dangled off the end of the fork was, *Is this rooster balls?* Better known as rooster testicles.

There were eight oval, pink, purple-veiny, testicle-shaped flesh balls attached in staggered formation by a pink, rubbery, tube-looking hunk of animal part. On one end, the rooster balls were centimeter-long. On the other, they were almost chicken-egg-sized. *What the hell is this? Is this a joke to be pulled on the foreigner at the table? Like, will he eat rooster nuts because he doesn't know nothing about nothing?*

I glanced around. Blanca was there saying something to me in Spanish. Maria was also there and saying something to me in Spanish. I held the animal part out on the fork. It looked wretched. I turned my gaze to the women. It should be without saying I didn't want to offend anyone. So, I eyed up my meal and gave it serious thought. *Do I put it in my mouth?* I also thought, *If I hold it on my fork just a couple seconds longer, they won't be able to hold a straight face, and the joke will expose itself.*

Just then, Maria motioned for me to slide the bowl

across the table to her. She took hold of it, dipped her spoon right in, and started eating the balls. I was embarrassed. At that exact moment, I knew that I unknowingly had been offensive. I could see it on Maria's face. I could sense that she knew I was a wuss. I had acted as a too-good-to-eat-their-food American snob. And worse, I knew it too. It pained me that I didn't have the vocabulary to ask them what the food was or explain what I thought it was.

When Maria took a bite of the mystery food, it became apparent what she was eating. These weren't rooster testicles. They were chicken eggs without shells. The inside of the largest ball looked exactly like a hard-boiled egg. Further research taught me that hens have an internal conveyor belt of eggs forming at all times—even if unfertilized. The small ovals were immature eggs, and the large ovals were eggs at the stage just before the hen's body begins creating a shell over them. This whole culinary contraption was the reproductive tract of a hen. I had never, ever been exposed to anything like it.

Interacting with Maria was the ultimate in seeing who I was when trying to be respectful while having no idea as to what could be offensive to someone. If needed, I always could activate a submissive nature when reading a situation, just like a dog rolling on its back. When I didn't know what Maria wanted of me, I summoned Mr. Ultra-Nice. This time, it mostly worked, but she was visibly annoyed. So, a few days later, it came as a surprise that Maria wanted me to join in on a walk around Macas.

She was eighty-four then. From Alice, I gained word

that Maria had been ill for some time. During my stay, I didn't know what her ailment was. I could hardly tell anything was ailing her. She had shown me vigor during the soup incident. She moved around well and had the energy for multiple attempts to talk to me. Her walking with us, in her condition, was proof of her character, humility, and love as a beautiful woman and mother. A year after this journey, I'd learn that Maria passed from cancer.

Maria decided she'd guide Blanca and me on a complete tour of Macas. I imagined she wanted to lead the way so she'd see her city's favorite places. As we walked, Blanca gave it her best to explain what the things were that we looked at. Between us, we knew a couple dozen words of each other's language. Her favorite English word was her name. She knew that it translated to white, and she'd laugh about it. I'd already caught Lucia and Angel calling her "White," just for the fun of it.

We roamed through the city square. It was the same one that, a few nights before, was glowing with Christmas lights. We wandered down a long and wide paved street, where small green leaves were floating in a line across the road. As we approached the leaves, I made out that each leaf had a dutiful ant attached to it. These were leaf-cutter ants—the same ones I'd seen on TV over the years. From afar, the leaves looked like tiny sails crossing the street. And the ants had chewed them in somewhat triangular shapes with one side curved, just like a sail. Blanca pointed at the ants and said, ""hormigas." And just like that, I learned a new word. And it stuck. I found that words learned during the inspiration of discovery were easier to remember than words spoken during study or when read from a book.

The next word I learned during the walk knocked my socks off. It was volcan. Blanca said "volcan" as she lifted her arm and pointed her finger toward the corner of a house. I wasn't making sense of what she was doing. *Was the house a volcan?* I wondered. Then I thought, *Houses are casas. Is there a plant in the yard called a volcan? Am I not seeing an animal called a volcan?* She continued to point, and my eyes focused on the horizon. Thus, I discovered her intention. In the gap between two houses and twenty-seven miles away, I saw a life's first. It was a freaking volcano! *No way!*

Spotting a volcano on this walk was the last thing on my mind. It simply was anything but obvious what she was saying. Her Spanish pronunciation sounded like bollcon to my English ear. And with that, volcan became a word I'll never forget because of its moment of discovery, just like "hormigas.

We were looking at the 17,000-foot Sangay Volcano. From Macas, only its snow-capped peak was visible. The summit was so bright that it was camouflaged among the clouds and sky. Leaving West Virginia, the last thing I thought I'd see on the equator was snow. This was also the highest peak I'd ever seen. Wow! Few could be happier than me then.

The United States is home to several volcanoes. But I'd been coast to coast without seeing one. They're just not something you often think of when your home is within the Appalachians. Only thoughts of Hawaii had really brought any following thoughts of volcanoes. And I rarely thought of Hawaii. Of course, there was the

1980 Mt. Saint Helen's eruption in Washington State. It served notice to the country. I'd heard infrequent stories about it, but since, volcanoes were something I'd always wanted to see without them taking up much room in my mind.

The three of us wandered on. Children played in the streets, running, and laughing. Flowers grabbed most of our attention. One such flower belonged to a shrub-like Borrachero tree. It was an eight-inch, tubular, white flower that grew downward and flared out at its underside opening. I thought it looked like a sleek and tasteful wedding dress. There were slight, inch-long tails coming from the pedals, reminiscent of wedding dress frills. Blanca began to try to explain this flower's significance more than any other we'd seen.

I deciphered that this flower was highly toxic. She motioned with her hand, and a deep breath, as to inhale while saying "pollen" in Spanish. Pollen is nearly spelled the same in both languages, so I caught on. Afterward, her expression told me that this flower was dangerous. She was also able to share with me that it was used for robbing people.

Curiosity forced me to research the flower later. The flower of the Borrachero tree has seed pods that can be cracked open. The contents can be used to make a powder that a person might place on a business card and hand to another person. Inhalation of this powder causes temporary amnesia in the victim while also making them fully suggestible. Putting it bluntly, criminals will force you into contact with the powder, suggest you empty your bank account, or help load your belongings into their truck. When the zombification wears off, you're left questioning what happened. Both Ecuador and Colombia are known for this type of crime.

In the discovery of this flower, I reflected upon the flight to Ecuador and roofie girl. She may have come in contact with this powder. The drug is commonly known as burundanga in South America. The active ingredient is scopolamine, and it's more ominously known as devil's breath.

Later, the sun was setting. We were walking alongside Macas's tiny airport runway and near Lucia's home again. We had almost completed an entire circle around the city. On the other side of the airport's fence, a lone corn stalk sat silhouetted in the evening light. It had been mangled by something. It looked diseased. Each leaf was three times thinner than normal and sawtooth patterned. Blanca looked at me and said, ""hormigas." I was floored! It's possible that the line of ants we saw marching on the other side of town were carrying their leaf cuttings from this hopeless, lone cornstalk.

In a far less dramatic fashion, staying a few days with Lucia began to dismember me like the ants had done the corn. In what should have been a continuously captivating experience, and it mostly was, an old character flaw began to germinate within. Self-conscious thoughts crept into my awareness, so much that I approached Lucia with my laptop open and a translation service at the ready. A question needed to be answered. Is it time to head back to Vilcabamba now?

From the clearest information I had, Lucia said I could stay for as long as I wanted. What I was bothered by was, *I'm a burden because they have to feed and entertain me.* Maybe they didn't have to, but they had been. Moreover, they wouldn't let me wander Macas alone to find a place to eat. Another thought was bothering me: *Am I interrupting Lucia's ability to help her clients and earn money?* I wasn't sure, but it seemed so. She hadn't worked steadily during my first days there. Then there was the learned-from-experience thought: *No one stays with anyone this long in the States unless they live with them.* Between Alice and I, the boundary of visitation was clear. Our extensive exchanges in English proved that. Between Lucia and I, I hadn't a clue. When you don't speak the language, you live inside your head by fistfuls more percentage.

So, we hashed it out over the translator. When Lucia realized what I was wondering, she seemed a bit shocked and saddened. Her response was one of self-doubt—as if she, or her family, had done something wrong to cause me to want to leave early. How confusing it all was. I thought I'd already stayed too long, and she thought I hadn't stayed long enough. She had so much more for me to discover. The next few days would be incredibly confusing, wholesome, hilarious, and mind-blowing.

Speaking of the mind, I must bring light to the limits of mine. To figure if you're a genius or not, immerse yourself in a country, in a culture, in a family, or in a household that doesn't speak your language. Then, do not fail to realize how slowly you're able to learn their language. That's what humility feels like, mi amigos. It feels like confusion—unavoidable confusion.

But what does saying this prove? It proves that I'm

the median—an average human without an advanced edge for learning anything, especially a language. If I can wind up in Ecuador having a good time and making friends, anyone can. If you're staunchly opposed to immersing yourself in a situation like this, there will always be room for the argument that you're not a genius. You'd rather hold tightly to your own sheltering. The proof is in the test.

There's endless unintentional fun to be had with language barriers. For me, the fun began as early as first thing in the morning at coffee time. Simply getting a cup of coffee could start the day's adventure. In high simplicity, one morning Blanca and I walked to a completely ordinary grocery store to buy regular coffee. Instant coffee was all they had. *That's fine.* I bought it and moved forward. I could not verbally express my desire for regular, but it was okay.

Another morning, Josie accompanied me to a restaurant where I attempted to get a cup of regular coffee. The waitress brought out a cup of near-boiling water and some instant coffee powder in a jar. I went with it again. There was no problem. I wasn't a coffee snob. I took it that Macas was a city dry of regular ground coffee. Lucia's family, and perhaps most Ecuadorians, were tea-oriented folks.

Somehow, in the basic communication attempts between myself, Josie, and Blanca, the message was received that I hoped to find real coffee. There was an afternoon when Blanca came in the kitchen holding a bag of pale, green beans. She snagged my attention and said, "café." (coffee) I moved closer to inspect her find.

Blanca had gone to the town market and scored freshly husked, unroasted coffee beans. Their shape was a dead match. *This is interesting.*

Blanca began gathering cooking paraphernalia. She turned the stove on and put a clay pot on the heat. *Oh, she's planning to roast the green right out of these beans.* The beans went in. *Okay, very neat. Never saw this. She knows what's going on.* I was in my head thoroughly, with eyeballs all over the situation. She took a large spoon and stirred the beans. Then, she urged me to do the same. *Okay. I'm following.* The beans soon began to look like pre-ground coffee beans. They were browning. By golly, I was gonna have real coffee the next morning! This was exciting.

Then things zigged when they should have zagged. Blanca asked me, "¿Azucar?" (Sugar) I was confused. Why was she asking about sugar? I took this as small talk and agreed. I replied, "Si. Azucar." (Yes. Sugar) I thought she was asking if I drank my coffee with sugar. I thought she might ask if I used cream next. But that wasn't her intention. She was looking for instruction rather than small talk. She went for a sugar container, dumping half a measuring cup's worth into the clay pot with the beans. *Uh oh!*

I didn't think for a second that would be her next move. And I wasn't fast enough to stop her. She was a train with momentum, and the language barrier made that a train with no brakes. That sugar was in the pot! She kept on stirring. I tried to tell her what happened, but unsuccessfully. The beans would be way too sticky to grind now. *What could we do?*

We kept stirring. The beans eventually roasted enough to use. The sugar darkened into a liquid. We stopped when we realized the beans were too sticky to smash into a technically usable pile of grounds. So, we moved forward with smiles. I'm not sure what Blanca thought of the whole situation. The next morning, I reverted to the instant coffee from the grocery store.

This confusion and surprise hit me again at Macas's outdoor food market. The gals and I went there seeking a twenty-inch-long seed pod called guaba. These guaba pods were novel. Inside them were inedible dark-brown seeds, larger than a lima bean but nearly the same shape. Those seeds were covered in a puffy filament that looked exactly like cotton. That white fluffy stuff was the edible part. To eat it, you'd finger out a seed, stick it in your mouth, then use your tongue and suction to finagle the filament off of the seed. Afterward, you'd spit the seed out. The white stuff was delicious and nearly as sweet as sugar. I looked forward to eating as many as I could get. That is until culture shock became part of the menu.

We found a stand selling the guaba. A teenage female handed us a few to inspect for freshness. She was made up well, rather pretty, and wearing clothes that would've been fashionable in the US. Nothing about her stood out as odd. I took hold of the guaba she handed me and cracked it open, lengthwise. With the first seed in hand, I noticed a brown spot a few inches from the end of the pod. This overly ripened brown area was the habitat for a wriggling, centimeter-long, brown-rice-colored larvae of some grotesque species. I pointed this out to the young lady.

Without hesitation, she snagged the guaba from me and fetched that larvae, putting it in her mouth. She was on to the next subject so fast that I hadn't had time to catch my breath. She looked at all of us like, "See? This is still a good guaba." Watching her eat that worm struck me hard. In my overly-privileged country, no fashionable teen girl is going to voluntarily eat a random worm. To me, her eating that thing looked like a shortcut to acquiring a parasite. "No gracias," was all I could muster. Surprises were many. Lucia was nowhere near done with me yet. I'd soon find out why during another supremely early morning kidnapping.

It began with another knock at the bedroom door, followed by a "Miiike," coming from Lucia. I may have been asleep for four hours. She came in and urged me to meet downstairs at a taxi. This time, I trusted we were going somewhere cool and out of harm's way. From what I gathered, it was a hot spring. I grabbed my camera, some money, and a jacket.

The taxi driver was a tired-looking young man named Julio. Lucia, Blanca, and Josie piled in the back. I was offered the co-pilot's seat. Once again, off we went into the night. I hadn't a clue which direction we were headed or how long the ride would be. I figured we may only travel a bit further than the dirt road that led to Mamita Virgin. *Just how long could a taxi ride be?*

Soon, Macas disappeared altogether. It was still plenty dark, and we seemed to be ascending. The road was paved and marked nicely. It weaved left and right vigorously like a fast-slithering snake. I was thinking,

This would be a phenomenal road for motorcycling!

Since we were ascending, we'd have to be heading West and back into the Andes. No matter the direction we were going, I began to really enjoy this ride. We passed through a couple mountain tunnels. Each one was far more rudimentary than almost any you'd find in the States. The lighting was low-tech, industrial, and the walls weren't always smooth concrete. There was one tunnel that began semi-smooth then became the jagged innards of a mountain, as if they had given up halfway through construction. It seemed far more like traveling through a mine than a roadway tunnel. My imagination played with the unfinished, bare rock walls until I whispered, "I feel like I'm inside a worm."

It was now early daylight. We pulled over after crossing a bridge. We were in the high mountains again. Below, a whitewater river rushed loudly through boulders on an expedited journey out of the Andes. After taking a moment for pictures, we continued onward. I was charged. The girls giggled a lot while our driver, Julio, was smiling and enjoying his day. Such dynamic environments are stimuli for the mood.

Now, the taxi windows were television screens to an invigorating outside world into which I was fully engaged. Everywhere I looked, it looked cool. Meanwhile, we continued to ascend. *Just how high are we going?* I wondered. A while later, we stopped again. We'd all climb out and frolic around on boulders at the base of a waterfall—a waterfall that was blasting straight out of a forest!

Looking up, the top of the waterfall was hidden

among the trees. Its stream of water appeared so suddenly and forcefully from the dense vegetation that it was like a magic trick being performed by nature. In all other waterfall encounters I'd had, I could clearly determine that the waterfall was coming from a particular river, creek, or stream. Not here, though. This waterfall was like the forest was taking a forceful yet beautiful pee.

We took some pictures and drove on. Another stop and the green Andes began to change. Greens had now blended with browns, while trees had passed the relay wand up the mountain to grasses and mosses. There wasn't a minute's drive since Macas, where we had not been ascending. If you'd ask me how high we were at this stop, I'd blurt out an unsophisticated, "10,000 feet!" I knew we were high, and finally, I knew somewhat of where we were. We'd just passed a sign that read, "Parque Nacional Sangay." (Sangay National Park) We were in high volcano territory.

Sangay National Park is a 2,000-square-mile home to two active volcanoes—Sangay and Tungurahua. It is also home to extremely rare mountain tapirs, spectacled bears, giant otters and jaguars, and little red brocket deer. It's listed as a United Nations Educational, Scientific and Cultural Organization (UNESCO) world heritage site. Nearly every climate the Earth offers is found in the park—from rain forests to glaciers. That day, it would be home to us.

To make a complete group of *us*, we'd meet Linda, Lucia's sister, at our next stop and turnaround point. We'd no longer ascend the winding road further above the tree line. Yet, we managed to arrive right at the foothills of heaven. Everything about this spot held majesty in a way that confused me as much as excited me. This very spot made me unapologetically want to use the word beautifuler. The hills were incomparable to any I'd seen in my life. These were hills that could influence the king of hillbillies to build his castle there.

We stood outside the taxi. A single-story, timber-framed building was in front of us. Its low-pitched roof was of thatched straw and looked of Shakespearean England. A three-inch-thick, handmade rope had been placed strategically on the straw to weigh it down. I guessed it was there to prevent the straw from blowing away. The gentle zig-zag pattern of the rope covered the entire roof. I had not seen this building technique before—ever.

Then an old man passed by on a horse. He was wearing what must have been handmade, loose, and layered clothing of colorful texture and character. His face showed a hardened life lived in its rugged mug. I was instantly bombarded with the thought, *God, I feel like I'm in Mongolia!* The highlands here demanded my attention with their stew of mixed landscapes. Here, nothing looked like the Ecuador I'd seen in Vilcabamba, Loja, or Macas.

Images of landscapes I'd experienced in the American West had congregated here. There was an enormous nearby outcropping that looked as though it had been chiseled and transplanted from Texas's Chisos mountains. It poked the sky with a commanding prominence like those landmarks seen in Arizona's

Monument Valley. And still, its rich, dark-chocolate soil color, of the same I'd seen on the canyon walls of Lake Mead, sparked yet another memory.

Between ourselves and the horizon, and under a big sky full of all the fresh mountain air a man could want, Wyoming's doppelganger laid before us. Rolling grassland spread miles in each direction, only interrupted by the horizon's almost fake-looking display of towering, Andean ridges—irrationally gorgeous, soaring ridges. California, Colorado, New Mexico, and Montana also came to mind here. It all had me wondering, *How the hell did I get here? And why was I so lucky?* I didn't know, but I knew if Lucia ever wanted to kidnap me again, she had my consent.

Mere moments before I became possessed by the land, and wandered off for good, I heard a few 'Mikes' coming from the women. They snapped me out of the spell. I had walked away from the group and to the edge of the grassland. I didn't notice Linda had arrived.

I followed the girls into the thatched-roof building. Again, my senses were boggled. This place's interior toyed with my imagination enough to feel like I was in merry-old, Spanish-speaking England. Hoisting my gaze straight at the ceiling revealed straw on the underside of the thatched roof. Darkened lumber, about the size of 2x8s, served as runners for the straw to lay. Heavy timber trusses supported those slats. Wood paneling, and a stone fireplace, gave me an instant thought of an old Irish pub. But an adjacent brick wall, painted pastel green, reminded me that I was in a Latin American country, and the desired vibe was positivity.

The place was a restaurant. And it was time to eat. The waitress greeted us and began taking orders. *Where's the menu?* By this time, my ability to decipher Spanish through reading was twice as good as speaking it. Spanish happens to be just similar enough to English so that if you approach it as if figuring out a code, the spelling of some words will give you an idea of what you're reading. Without a menu, I was as good as blindfolded for figuring out what was for sale there. I knew coffee. That's café. Salad is ensalada. Vegetables is vegetales. Juice is jugo. Fruits is frutas. See the similarities? But fish is pez in Spanish. In America, PEZ is a type of candy. I didn't want candy.

Josie and Blanca helped fill in the gaps between the waitress and me, and I wound up with pez. Specifically, a trout spread head to tail on a long, oval plate. The head and the tail were completely intact. Everything between had been fashioned into a salad of sorts. It looked kind of like this trout had swallowed a micro, veggie bomb.

As it laid there, one eye looked up at me. I'd be lying if I didn't feel somewhat guilty for that animal's death. The spoiled American within had only once before experienced an entire animal as a meal. That was at a pig roast. Until then, all other meats had arrived before my hungry mouth neatly packaged or shaped in a way as to not to look like an animal. Culturally, it's just a bit bizarre to make eye contact while you're chewing on an animal. I'm not a wolf, I say, as I mention the spoiled American within again.

The meal went perfectly. We were happy when we

returned to the outdoors to reengage with our surroundings. The very first thing that caught my eye outside was an eight-foot-wide, concrete waterhole stocked with trout. I'd somehow walked right past it going in. One look at those fish, and "You're next" came to mind. Romancing the world leaves no room for its honest operation. It's all give and take. Thank you, tiny trout, for being part of my experience in magnificent Sangay National Park.

Julio taxied us in the direction we came. But then, we parked again only after a mile. A look around, and we were in a wide, gravel lot. Surrounding us were a couple hardscrabble shacks. One was painted with that same pastel green as in the restaurant. And painted on it, by hand, was the word: "Restaurant." Maybe this was the former park eatery. We stopped there for the view.

The women led the way into a giant swath of field plumb full of knuckle-shaped hills. They were pointy and smooth and covered in dense clumps of grass. There were infinitely numerous stalks of delicate, long, blonde grass. Our panorama was one of unbothered mountain lakes like an American might picture in their mind of Alaska. Making the far border of this expanse was a supremely high-elevation range of Andes. They looked milk-chocolate brown and were treeless. They were jagged and remote and begged exploration.

We walked through a foot-wide trail in the hair-like grass. Up steep inclines and down matching descents, we went. These hills were shaped in a way that one could imagine a sky-scraper-sized dump truck dumping its load of soil and leaving smooth mounds of earth. The scenery took my breath in multiple ways. I noticeably breathed harder due to the elevation, and I was enamored with it. I followed Lucia to a stopping point, grinning all the while.

The women mingled while I gawked at this remarkable slice of mountain glory. If it were Wyoming, and we were out and exposed like this, I'd have wolves, or bears, or cougars on the mind. I'd be incredibly vigilant. But this was Ecuador. We were safe to have a little fun. They took pictures of themselves with that tremendous background to their rear. Their smiles and laughs were bright spots of essence drifting around among the hills. I don't know how they felt seeing Sangay National Park at that moment, but they sure seemed like they were seeing it for the first time, just like me.

We left that area, and Julio drove us another mile down the road with Linda following in her car. At this stop, a lake spread out below the road to our right. Most of the women stayed at the road surface. Josie and I hiked down a steep, rocky hundred-foot embankment. Her adventurous teenaged spirit urged her to come along. My inner-knowing desire to experience Zen had me carefully descending toward the lake. I had an eye on the rocky shore below.

Growing up on the banks of West Virginia's Shenandoah River, I gained a seemingly trivial skill at a very young age. My father taught me how to skip rocks along the surface of water. Almost magically, I'd watch him find a flat rock and throw it, underhandedly, toward the river. His arm would swing whip-like as the rocks defied all logic. How could something as dense as a rock bounce off of something as non-supportive as water? Again and again, the rocks would spin and bounce and spin and bounce. He'd excitedly look for another rock.

Nowadays, seeing the physics of rock skipping come to life temporarily births a valuable and welcomed quiet mind. I've also felt this sensation staring at the ocean and staring at the dance of campfire flames. Skipping rocks has always been something I've taken time to do.

Although, I don't think Josie had taken that time. We were lakeside and hunting for good skippers. I had a sharp eye searching for a flat one, and Josie would pick up a chunky one, then call my name. Looking me in the eye, she sought confirmation on that rock's skipability. I'd laugh and urge her to go for it. Sometimes, she'd pull off a two or three-jumper. When I'd find a good flat geologic gift, I could get ten or more swift skips.

We'd hear the gals up at the road congratulate me on those tosses. Julio was feeling the vibe and had climbed down to the lake to join us. From the left, I saw a rock blaze across the surface. One, two, three, four, five, six, seven skips! Our young taxi driver was a pro. How fantastic to see this! He had the technique perfected.

It's a far trickier technique than imagined. I've seen many try unsuccessfully. They'd get the underhand toss but not the wrist flick. Or they'd get the wrist flick but fail to release the rock when it's parallel to the water's surface, making it sink straight in. Or they'd not realize that so much lies in the backspin and the subtle placement of the pointer finger for making that backspin.

Josie and I kept hunting for the perfect stones among the thick, square, and sharp-edged ones the lake was offering. These were unlike the plentiful, smooth, and flat ones of my home. Once, I was on the hunt for a good rock near the water's edge and fell off a boulder. I dabbed a shin in the lake. Josie laughed! A few times, I got a dozen skips while Josie kept trying. We had skipped so many rocks and were altogether in the zone. Time had to have passed differently for us and our friends up at the road. For me, it couldn't have lasted long enough. For our friends, three youthful spirits were getting way too caught up in such basic activity.

Josie and I couldn't consistently speak five words to one another. Still, I was nearly insane with happiness for being brought to this national park by Lucia. I don't know if she sensed it or not, but inside me, an energy that could only be known as happiness warmed my soul. That day, and especially, skipping those rocks on the shore of that lake with Josie, will be cherished until I die as one of the purest moments of my life.

Into the Amazon

There are some plans you don't tell your mother until you've survived them. Minutes ago, we entered a white-out of clouds in a tiny aircraft. We were a few hundred feet over the last bit of hills of the Eastern Andes and flying into the Amazon Jungle. The pilot had been angling the plane to the right to avoid two angry, red blobs on his navigation tablet. Our course would have normally been a rather straight shot from Macas to a runway somewhere in the flat jungle to the east. But today, our pilot was trying to thread the needle.

    The storm was rogue in its desire to share its winds and rain with us. It matched our pace and southeast direction nearly equally. On the navigation screen, the blue dot representing the plane moved as slowly as a snail would move if it crawled across that same screen. The insignificance of the tiny dot shown clearly while flanked and fleeing from the giant morphing reds.

Can we go fast enough to outrun the storm? The pilot sure thought so. He saw a gap in the blobs and figured he could make it. I was concerned. *How the heck could we be flying in such conditions?* When I looked down, I could see the sixteen-inch balloon tire on the right side of the plane. I couldn't see anything else. I prayed those blobs wouldn't merge and engulf us. I'd never been so nervous in flight.

The pilot's gamble paid off. Now, the storm trailed behind us. When the clouds cleared, a tree canopy that looked like fields of broccoli florets dominated the view far below. A snaking, muddy river was running heavy with chocolate-milk-colored water. It contrasted highly in the endless green. We were headed somewhere vastly different than what I'd seen in the high-elevations and foothills of the Andes. A hint of civilization would've been as welcome as a cold beer with a good friend. I was about to encounter yet another telescopic extension of the oh-shit stick away from my comfort zone.

We spotted the runway. It was much more a pasture than a runway. Dense, healthy, foot-high grass welcomed the plane back to the surface of the Earth. I was happy for touchdown but nowhere near comfortable. We were experiencing a bumpy ride down a runway, going way faster than a goofy-looking small plane with tiny wheels should be going. A Baja race truck might be better suited for such speed on a jungle runway. And just when we began to slow, and I felt like there was no chance I'd die, we plowed through standing water that splashed skyward and covered the side windows. The plane handled it all remarkably well.

I followed Celine, my travel companion, out of the plane. We'd arrived deep in the Western Amazon. We barely knew one another. Moreover, we definitely didn't know the folks walking from the jungle and across the runway toward us. This bizarre string of events began the night before when I agreed to fly into the jungle with a stranger from Switzerland.

Through an online translator, Lucia told me that she'd soon introduce me to her English-speaking friend, Hanna. Hanna was a Swiss woman living in Macas. Years before, Hanna's husband had taken an interest in Ecuador's native Shuar people of the Western Amazon. And so, they moved to Macas. After his death, she remained as quite possibly the lone, white, English-speaking person in the city. Lucia probably thought it was good for my psyche to have a chance to talk like a normal human for a couple hours. So, one evening we went across town to visit Hanna.

Surprising both Lucia and me, Hanna's long-estranged niece, Celine, was visiting from Switzerland. Celine and Hanna had just returned from a tour of the Galapagos Islands. The women were charged with adventurous energy. Both told us of their experiences, as both had a strong command of English and Spanish. I'd always loved meeting the intrepid souls who take the time to travel this world, no matter their reason. Lucia's intuition that led her to introduce me to Hanna was deeply appreciated. I had reactivated my native tongue in conversation. However, neither Lucia nor I intuited an adventure the next day involving an airplane. We found out about that after having returned to Lucia's.

At nine p.m., Hanna called Lucia, and I was directed to take the phone. Hanna excitedly poured out a plan for me to accompany Celine on a prearranged trip to stay with the Shuar tribe. My mind nearly locked up once she laid out the details. I was thinking, *Small plane, giant jungle, anacondas, jaguars. I may die.* For me to say this sounded great is as bold-faced a lie as any that could be told. But I went for it.

I had made it this far by blindly fumbling through Ecuador. Why not say "yes"? If anything, chivalry could have been conjured as a legitimate reason. If I didn't agree to go, Celine would have to go alone. What kind of man would let that happen? Agreeing to go in the face of my thick, self-preservative, better judgment was my only choice. I'd meet Celine at the airport in the morning.

Now, here we were on the runway at the end of the flight. I'm out of the plane with a bag of clothes in hand. I'm wearing a floppy fishing hat and blue jeans. There's a camera strap over my shoulder, and I'm looking as out of place as an upside down letter. People were walking from all directions across the runway to meet us. All of them were young children and late teens.

One was a mother with a child strapped tightly to her back by a heavy brown cloth. Her toddler's legs hung free down to her waist. She and her relatives were wearing rather normal clothes. They had on tee-shirts of random name brand, shorts, and muck boots. Albeit much of their clothes were more worn and lived-in looking than the mainstream.

Their skin was a few shades darker than most of the

other Ecuadorians I'd met. This could have come simply from living outside and having more exposure to the sun. The young mother's face was absent of European influence, unlike many Ecuadorians. She did have high cheekbones, a strong jawline, and perfect symmetry, making her rather pretty. There was another young mother there too. And she was the same. I noticed their facial structure was slightly different than other Ecuadorians, as well. Their eyes were somewhat further apart. They were open wide and more alert, crisper, and a darker brown—the complete opposite of my narrow, beady blues. This helped give the first impression of a focused nature.

Only one of the young mothers smiled when meeting us. I think that was due to Celine's encouragement. She had her camera out and was pressing them for pictures. These folks were fairly quiet. I gave thought to their quietness as potentially being a good or bad thing.

A young man offered to carry my bag. Another took Celine's. I allowed him to do so, knowing that he was probably sent to do so. Otherwise, I'd have preferred to carry it myself. It was a nice gesture. But any traveler could tell you that there's something about handing your goods off to strangers that strikes a primal gut reaction. Possibility number one is, everything goes fine, and my stuff is handed back to me when we get to wherever the heck we're going. Possibility two, my stuff is gone through and shared with the village when we get to wherever the heck we're going. I knew so little about the coming experience that my guard was high enough to take the fun out of it. I was incredibly deep inside my head.

Celine seemed to be taking it in stride and taking even more photos. Neither one of us knew these people, yet Celine had the gumption to force photos on them moments after stepping out of the plane. She often had her camera a foot or two from their faces. I saw this as rude. *How can she not pick up on their reserved nature?* I questioned.

Looking around, there was a lone shed at the runway. I think it had some sort of phone in it. That was the only way this trip made sense to me. Maybe Hanna called someone at the runway shed to arrange our arrival. In the broader periphery, it was all dense jungle. Vines hung from trees; broad palm-like leaves fanned out among a full spectrum of shades of green. We were directed to follow these young folks into the forest. This was unexpected.

My heightened anxiety demanded I notice everything around me. The path we walked began with slabs of wood to form somewhat of a footing and edge. Most of these were sunk deep into the mud. As we moved onward, they disappeared. Then, we stepped and sank and slipped in the rainforest mud. The trail narrowed to a little more than the width of a human. Celine was ready at the camera in front of me. I brought up the rear. Plants dwarfed us on either side.

We were a couple hundred yards in when we came to an absolutely massive tree. I stopped dead in my tracks to appreciate its size. Everyone else moved on as if it weren't abnormal, even Celine. I commented on the tree's size just to slow them down so I could look at it. The trunk of this tree rivaled most giant coastal redwoods I had seen. Fifty feet up its height, it was still twelve feet in diameter. Even weirder, its lower trunk was wildly different than any tree trunk I'd ever seen.

Below the trunk's giant cylinder of wood was fanned-out, above-ground ribbons of wood. This made for a much wider diameter and less bulky appearance at the tree's ground level. These trunk ribbons are known as buttress roots. I had no verbal ability to know the species of this behemoth in the moment. Research, later, would lead me to guess with near certainty that it was a Kapok Tree. Some specimens of the Kapok have been measured with nineteen-foot trunk diameters and sixty-five-foot buttress root diameters. They're capable of towering to 240 feet. Coming across this tree greatly excited me for the surprises that lay ahead in this adventure into the Amazon.

The momentary amazement faded the further we walked. I arrived back in the world of caution inside my head as we approached a clearing. *This must be where we're headed.* To our right was a steep hillside. Celine and I followed on up it. Crossing the top and looking around, I noticed four quintessential huts. They were built of native timber, rudimentary in every way. All were kept dry inside by thatched roofs. Their walls were tightly constructed of vertical sticks positioned side by side. There were no doors. Nor were the walls impervious to light or wind.

Next, I noticed people scattered among the huts. Our walking guides joined them to make a family unit of maybe fifteen. We were greeted by a man named Jose. He was the family's father and leader. I will not refer to him as an elder or chief. I was unsure of the position they'd describe for themselves. And Jose didn't look very old. He may have been my age or minimally older. Celine was certainly older than him, at fifty-four years old. We soon found that ten of the more youthful people hanging around were his and his wife Pamela's children. Among them were very young grandchildren, belonging to Jose's oldest son.

Jose had thick, black, wavy hair kept in a fashion not far from a short 70's fro. He was a stout-looking man of perhaps five-foot-eight inches tall. His wife, Pamela, shared in the naturally pretty looks that I'd noticed in the two young mothers that had just hiked in with us. Jose proudly introduced all of his children. I took note of their names on a pad of paper, which I later lost in time. Somewhat surprisingly, Jose's oldest son was way stouter than his father. This young, jungle-dwelling man was as fit and muscular as any beach-bodied gym rat that tries to sell you supplements in infomercials.

I was taken aback by the young man's appearance. I knew better not to piss him off. He had to be twice as strong as me and definitely good with a machete. *How the hell did he get that way? Was he literally doing push-ups and squats all day, or was it simply genetic?* I hadn't noticed other Ecuadorians being naturally built like that. I once spent months doing that P90X program and didn't wind up close to that muscular.

In the very lowest of ages of Jose's grandchildren, I

found great intrigue by the way they looked at me. Celine's experience with them seemed lighter than mine. Celine seemed to be getting on with everyone just fine. She was a picture-taking freak. She was on a mission to capture every face, the huts, the moments—all of it. On top of that, she was interacting with the toddlers and attempting to make them smile for good photographs.

That is not my nature. I'm an observer. I have a file cabinet for a brain, and I'm somewhat walled-off to interactions that pull me away from that nature. These toddlers were starkly afraid of me. I am tall, and that could have been the first indication of their fear. I may have been the tallest human they'd seen. I am a redhead through and through. My hair might have thrown them off. But deep down, their God-given innocent appraisal of me was that I was a weird-looking, something or other humanoid.

They were young enough that this could have been their first interaction with a true white man. It was not lost on me the bizarreness they probably felt. I'd feel the same way staring at a Bigfoot. On top of that, I am extremely pale-skinned. And worse, that pale skin was recently scorched by the sun during that outing at Sangay National Park. I'd spent the whole day at the park, exposed to the sun and without sunscreen.

Now, my face was peeling skin in the company of these children, and those kids freaking knew it. They'd back away from me as if I was diseased with nothing but the purest of concerned looks on their faces. I could imagine them thinking that I lost all of my color from an illness. It seemed as if they were instinctively alarmed. Their eyes weren't giving me a moment's breath to relax without their innocent judgment. Three of them never warmed to me during our entire stay.

There was one structure as out of place as me in their tiny village. It was an elevated gathering place of sorts, like a roof-covered deck. It sat about three feet off the ground and was the only structure built with dimensional lumber. I'd guess it was twelve by twenty feet long. We were invited to walk onto it and have a seat.

I was a sweaty mess from the hike and totally ignorant of what I should be doing. I've always been generous with a smile, so I defaulted to that to get by. Celine was mingling as if these folks were her family. Then one of the young mothers approached with a wooden bowl of cream-colored soup. She made an offer by extending it toward me. Without hesitation, I grabbed it and consumed it. My thought being, *Eat and drink what they offer. Do what they ask of me. And that shall keep my head on my shoulders.*

I must not leave out that the Shuar people are the Amazonian tribe specifically known for head shrinking. It's a practice less commonly used in modern times. When head shrinking was more prolific, it happened during warring among local tribes. The heads of fallen enemies would be shrunken and retained for their believed access to the power of the victim's soul.

I drank of the bowl of soup she offered, and Celine did too. We were both unaware of its ingredients. And given the heat and humidity, the soup's ambient temperature, and its general thickness, it's better off we didn't know. Especially me. I am cursed with a weak stomach. I've never been a picky eater. I just become nauseous easier than most. As a boy, I was the one who couldn't spin in circles at the pinata, or ride spinning rides at the carnival, or roll down the grassy hill with his friends. Doing these activities led me to the edge of vomiting way too soon. Injuries with blood and deformity sometimes cause me to pass out. And vomit, and things as wretched as vomit, cause me to vomit.

Here in Amazonia, what we were dealing with was chicha. We'd been offered, and had readily consumed, fermented spit beer. This chicha happened to be one of the specific things in life that I promised myself as a travel-interested man that I'd avoid if ever given the opportunity to consume it.

Chicha is a beer made by one of the cleverer tricks of nature—the kind that makes you wonder how the first person figured it out. Beer is a simple thing to make, given you have the ingredients. For chicha, you need the manioc plant, popularly known as yuca, boiling water, and the ptyalin enzyme that's released from a human's mouth.

By chewing the starchy yuca plant, and spitting out the contents into a collection vessel, the starch of the yuca becomes maltose. Later, a naturally occurring, airborne yeast begins a spontaneous fermentation as it devours the sugar in the liquid. My stomach spun a circle when I later found out what we had drank.

The offerings kept coming, and Celine and I drank until we'd had enough. It was hit or miss as to when to decline their offer. During the drinking, the young mother would serve me the chicha but look hard to her left as I drank. I was oblivious to why, simply thinking she's maybe laughing with her family as I drank the mystery soup.

Celine later asked, "Do you know why she looked away as she served you?" I said, "No. Why?" She said, "If a Shuar woman looks directly at a man while he drinks chicha, then she wants to sleep with him." It wasn't surprising to me that she looked away. That's been my life experience with women. I don't have those Brad Pitt looks. My looks are part leprechaun, with another thirty percent leprechaun.

The chicha welcoming ended, and we were set to do that for which we came. Hanna had somehow arranged an expedition into the jungle to see something she thought we'd love. We'd be guided by Jose for who knows how long to God knows where. Pardon my vagueness, but that was the knowledge with which I was traveling. Much like any incident with Lucia, I was just along for the ride.

Jose gathered Celine and me. Three of his young sons wanted to tag along. The group of us traded the village for a trail directly into the forest. In a couple hundred feet, we crossed a wood-plank, swinging bridge. Then, we traded that last bit of infrastructure for a leaf-covered path. We followed easily. The ground beneath was of squishy mud. Plants prodded into the air space of the path. Jose had his machete working immediately to clear small branches and large leaves. This was a path not often used.

We crossed a fallen tree. Jose and the boys went right under. Celine and I did too. But we were laden with bulky cameras and not accustomed to walking in muck boots. I had a fishing hat on and struggled to duck low enough with the awkward boots and camera swinging near the ground. I felt like such an infantile tourist as I tried to keep the tree from knocking my hat off, keeping the camera from getting wet, and my jeans and hands from going into the mud. I was a bit tall for going under it, but they waited. I believe this might have been the first look from Jose as to express, "Come on, man. Really?"

The precautions I took to stay somewhat clean and dry were deemed obsolete a few minutes down the path. The group arrived at the first river crossing. This one wasn't too bad. It was shallow, rocky, and mildly swift. Jose intuited we'd like to keep our cameras dry. He asked us to give him our cameras. We did, and he led the way into the water, holding our cameras high. I saw this as the exact right thing to do. He knew this river and had the footing in his muscle memory. He was aware of any underwater obstacles the same way I was at home in my native Shenandoah River. This time, I didn't mind being a low-grade tourist. It was smart.

On the opposite riverbank, I noticed the path regress to next to nothing. We were already walking a course that made the Appalachian Trail look like a highway. Now, we were walking a memory inside Jose's mind. He knew the way without a path.

We'd follow, and he'd make it a point to show us this species or that species of plant. He showed us the infamous combination of vine and leaf that the local shamans used to brew the world's most potent natural hallucinogen, ayahuasca. Of course, neither plant was near the other. If he'd not pointed them out, I would've passed by without a thought. We were in the world of plants. We were on their turf. Here in the Amazon, their botanical population density was like that of humans in Bangladesh.

It was impossible to follow the group without being poked by the thought of a jaguar ambush. I was bringing up the rear. A person couldn't see forty feet into the forest. The undergrowth sailed to the canopy in an uninterrupted wall of green. I trusted Jose knew the ways of the animals here, and I kept my mind not far from my four-inch pocketknife.

There was a section of trail made of large boulders. Some were nearly fifteen feet in diameter. All were salamander-skin slippery. Jose crossed them like a billy goat. Celine struggled a bit here. I helped her with a hand, noting that the rubber on our muck boots wasn't designed for climbing mossy boulders. As I held her hand, she unknowingly stabilized me. We were better at climbing as a team. A fall here, and we'd land in swift rapids, but we really weren't all that high.

Along the path, we managed to cross the river five times. Sometimes the water was nipple deep. *Wherever we are going, it must be good. This hike has been awesome by itself!* We'd neared the three-hour mark when we came to a broad and calm location in the river. I didn't know if this was another river crossing or our terminus.

Jose expressed that this was it. While looking around, it was quite evident this could be why we had come. Just blasting right out of the jungle were three waterfalls. Each one was only twenty feet high. But when I realized that two of them were steaming hot, my world changed with a surge of intrigue and a giant smile! "Hot waterfalls? What the heck is a hot waterfall?"

We flew in a plane from a tiny city in eastern Ecuador into the jungle, drank some beer soup, hiked for three hours through ayahuasca country with a man who comes from a head-shrinking lineage, all to discover another fantastic trick up the sleeve of mother nature. Here, she had said, "Heck, all waterfalls don't have to be cold. How's about I make some hot ones. This oughta give 'em humanzees a rise!" And Mother Nature laughed! And it was done.

I could not have been in greater appreciation for Hanna for this trip, or for Celine for inviting me to join, or for Lucia for introducing me to Hanna, or for Jose for hosting and guiding us. And to God and Mother Nature for their creation. It's incredibly easy to see how I could have made it an entire lifetime without knowing the existence of hot waterfalls. Their existence hadn't owned a millisecond of thought in the thirty-five years that I'd lived. The only connection I'd made to natural hot water were the geysers of Yellowstone, which I'd never seen in person.

This section of river brought to mind a lagoon. Where each river crossing had been swift and narrow, this area was pool-like—perhaps because of its width. It was twice as wide as many of the sections we had already crossed. The hike had been all upriver. Now looking further up-river, the water continued around a sharp bend made by a thick, plant-covered rock outcropping. The hot waterfalls met the cool river water here. That combination made for hanging mist. The fact that we couldn't see upriver meant that the jungle was a complete wall of green all around. The waterfalls demanded all attention and left me comparing this spot to the enchanting look of the forests in the movie *Avatar*.

I took my shirt off, exposing the Amazon to arguably the whitest skin thus far in that neck of the woods. I lunged forward in the shallow water and floated to the nearest hot waterfall. This one was not as free-falling as the other two. Those seemed to fall right out of the plants hanging twenty feet above the water. This one was amazing in that the hot water had left an outlandishly bright, orange deposit of minerals on the rock's surface. The water fell forcefully, splashing hard off the protruding parts of the stone. It was hot enough to be painful had I been fully immersed under it.

With this waterfall, the sweet spot was a foot off the rock. We'd catch the splash just so that it would feel like a hot shower with excellent water pressure. Jose's young sons really enjoyed being in and around this waterfall. It's safe to say they had never experienced a hot shower in a house after a long day's work. Yet here, nature had allowed them a day at the spa.

Celine was as tickled as I was, but I don't think she was as surprised. Who knew the conversation she and

Hanna had before I was invited? Jose seemed in his element and did a light bit of washing off in the other hot waterfall. In time, I waded over there to check it out. That hot waterfall was only five feet from another waterfall. One had a heavier flow, while the other fell with the strength of a couple kitchen faucets. Little did I know, one was hot, but I'll be damned if one wasn't cold! At my height, I could stretch my hands wide enough to have one hand in a cold waterfall and one hand in a hot waterfall at the same damn time. Activate mind expansion, I say. Who knew this was possible?

Since both were free-falling out of seemingly, well, plants, there were no mineral deposit clues from afar to show us that one was hot, and one was cold. It's fantastic to know that two flows of water traveled through a rock from two different sources so close. Still, they did not mix. The hot was very hot, and the cold was very cold. There wasn't a bit of heat in it.

Jose was right beside me when he said, "¿Listo?" I looked at him, smiled, and said, "Si." Then, I went back to being amazed and swimming around. A couple minutes later, he repeated it. I did the same thing again. And it happened again another time. Then he grabbed Celine's attention and said it to her. She looked at me and said it's time to go. I had confused listo with lindo. I thought Jose was asking me if the place was pretty, and I was replying, "Yes." But he had been asking me if I was ready—which is listo. Lindo is pretty in Spanish. The confusion couldn't quell my mood. I was happy, and even more, riding the train of good fortune.

While swimming, I concluded that I was in the most

remote place I had ever been. If a man from the outside world finds these waterfalls without the help of the Shuar, he's in serious trouble. The closer we got to them, the less of a trail there was to follow. The time we went over the boulders, there was no trail at all. Each time we crossed a river, you couldn't spot a trail continuing on the other side. We followed in blind faith in Jose. Should you discover these falls without him, you stand no chance of rescue. If we'd had slipped off a boulder and broken an ankle, there's but one way in and one way out—that trail. I'd surely never been a flight, and a three-hour hike into the wilderness in the US.

    We left the lagoon going in the same direction as we came. We had our hiking legs broken in, and the river crossings were somewhat easier. We were soaked from swimming, so there was no need to tiptoe. Celine really gave attention to capturing some of the birds of the jungle on our way back. Her camera was of way better quality than mine. It could focus instantly and not miss birds as they quickly flew by. My photos of the birds looked like bird-colored blobs in a backdrop of green. I was using a Canon Rebel T2i. It was expensive for my blue-collar status, selling at $800 retail the day I purchased it. It was perfect for stills, but its autofocus lagged for millisecond shots.

    Dusk had fallen at our return. Celine mingled with Jose's folks, and I took some time to record a video near a creek where, earlier in the day, I saw the women bathing their infants. Afterward, I was pulled aside by Jose so he could show me, quite proudly, two thirty-gallon drums of chicha that he had fermenting. I looked with a smile and could only think, *Good for you, my friend. I may not want anymore, but good for you for having plenty of what you enjoy!*

As night came, we gathered on the village's covered deck. Celine showed off her photos from the day to the little ones and allowed them to pass her camera around. They showed great delight in seeing themselves on its screen. I found it highly welcoming and surreal to observe these children interacting with her camera. They weren't of the selfie culture. Nor would this interaction with technology be taken for granted. Their smiles were tremendous!

We were served dinner shortly after. I was again supremely challenged to man up in the face of food. My queasy stomach nearly caved in on itself when they handed me the plate. Eight ugly fish were lying there, freshly boiled. They had all of the genetic beauty of a booger. For their body size, their scales looked far too large. Their color was that of mud. Their eyes were beady, and their oversized mouth was on the underside of the body. They had an aggressive, spiked dorsal fin that appeared ready for war. What we had here were eight-inch-long, sucker-mouthed, armored catfish.

I looked around, hoping to follow Celine's lead. But she wasn't stoked on them either. Neither one of us knew what to do with them. So, I took my dirty fingernails and dug in, peeling scales off. Sure enough, the back meat was brilliant white and easy to get. The fish fell apart nicely from being boiled. I grabbed a hunk and threw it past my threshold of teeth. It tasted kind of great! The second bite confirmed it wasn't much different tasting than crab meat. This was motivating for the thought of eating the rest of them. Accompanying the fish were thick, boiled strips of yuca. For his means, Jose had given us an obvious delicacy and a hearty dinner to replenish the energy used on the day's hike.

Celine and I were grateful for the surprise in the moment. For the life of me, I love variety and the novelty of other cultures. But is it impossible to not judge a book by its cover once in a blue moon? Celine and I sure did with those fish. Again, I'm not a picky eater, as there are only four things I've found I won't eat: butterscotch hard candy, black licorice, sauerkraut, and olives. Those flavors assault my tongue. I would've definitely eaten that reproductive tract at Lucia's, had I known it was only eggs. But that's it since even weird-looking fish are part of the menu now.

It was getting late, and these folks were up-with-the-sun people. Jose showed us which hut we'd stay in. Inside, there were two cots made from branches. We brought a little bit of gear to suffice as blankets. Surely it wasn't cold. Celine took a cot on one end and I, the other. Between us was a fire for keeping the bugs away. Their method for fire keeping was novel. They kept coals hot in the middle of three logs, positioned in a Y formation. As the ends would burn, they'd close the gap by pushing them closer. This was vastly different than piling logs on top of one another like I had always done.

In the dark and quiet of the evening, Celine and I spoke about the day. She was happy that I came, but she was surprisingly upset that I wasn't more open and adventurous in nature. She was correct in one aspect. I'm often too reserved, with a dose of easy-going—especially when I'm sober. For her, it was impossible to feel my internal gratitude and how it didn't take much to make me gracious. So, she determined that I wasn't being enough of something.

Basically, we had a spat about her thinking I wasn't man enough. In her mind, I should have been Bear Grylls in each situation the day had thrown at us. Often, I didn't lead. I didn't initiate conversation with Jose's family. I was squeamish about eating the fish. I was nervous on the plane. She was upset over things like that. Her saying it kind of blindsided me. I was just happy to be there and trying not to wind up in a situation for which a helicopter can't come whisk a person to a hospital.

She never did find out how rude it seemed, to me, that she'd shove her camera in these stranger's faces. She didn't know how pompous her Swiss mannerisms made her look. I'd never lower myself to her level of rudeness by telling her. Why chance ruining her once-in-a-lifetime experience? I wish she would've given me the same respect.

This led to barely any sleep on my end. At three a.m., a rooster began crowing just outside our hut's stick walls. It crowed until daybreak. I never fell back to sleep. Celine and I weren't old friends who'd get over it quickly. We were travelers just winging it. She got me on this adventure. I got her.

To Civilization

Morning came with a plan to leave at seven a.m. Jose met us at the hut to collect payment for the prearranged hike. The cost was twenty American dollars each. We gladly gave him that. But then, he unexpectedly requested more. This led Celine, or maybe the nature of the Swiss in her, to somewhat fly off the handle. She saw it as, *A deal's a deal.* I saw it as, *What's the big deal?* Jose might have assumed we had more money than we did. This was highly embarrassing behavior on her end. I convinced her to pay him a little more, stating I'd go half without a problem.

Jose was not a tour guide. He had never run a touring business. He was simply an acquaintance of Hanna's who had stopped whatever he was doing to host us weird gringos. He gave us an obvious delicacy, that someone had to catch fresh, and a place to sleep. An extra twenty was worth it. But the Swiss are the Swiss, I'd learn.

They're neat, orderly, and not very flexible. I observed it as a mentality. Jose ended up with the extra twenty. And if I had had more money on me, he'd have had twenty more on top of that. I didn't bring all of my cash into the jungle. It was left at Lucia's.

Thankfully, all was soon resolved. Celine and I were packed and following Jose, and his wife, out of the village to a different trail. We had to meet a young man who'd take us four hours downriver by canoe. That's where the nearest road was. And that's where we'd meet a taxi back to Macas.

The trail was short, and as they are in the Amazon, perpetually muddy. In ten minutes, we were on the bank of a different river than yesterday's hike. Celine and I climbed into the canoe. We expressed thanks many times to Jose and Pamela. Smiles were easily shared between us. The money issue didn't make it this far. Yet, a feeling was there that we were all glad it was over. As we pulled away, Jose gave a wave and a hearty, "Adios!" In my time in Ecuador, I learned that when a native Spanish speaker uses adios, he doesn't plan to see you again. If he did, he'd use one of many other salutations like, hasta luego, ciao, or hasta la próxima. Those are less permanent, culturally.

So began another wild adventure within an adventure. We were now in a gas-powered canoe. I thought it had possibly been fashioned from a log. I couldn't confirm this, but with the giant Kapok trees available, it's possible this canoe was carved from an old tree trunk. The river was wide and muddy and swift-flowing. The engine was powerful, and our young captain was a quiet sort. Somewhat immediately, everything from the past day got locked into a happy file in my brain, and I was present with the boat ride. Celine was enjoying this change of pace, too.

The riverbanks were fiercely uninterrupted by vegetation. Here and there, we'd see a bird. One bird was large and brown. To me, it looked like a chicken; although, it looked more exotic. I think it was a hoatzin. We spooked the thing, and it responded by flying away in a cumbersome fashion, just like a chicken, and landing on a thin branch. The branch swayed dramatically up and down with its weight.

There were plentiful Kapok trees towering among the rest. Again, I loved seeing their stature and feeling the surprise of realizing that the Amazon has giant trees. We weaved and wandered from riverbank to riverbank. The young man was reading the flow of the river for efficiency. When we came to rapids, he'd take us the safest way through. Those were always exciting, knowing an accident here might lead to death. Who knows what was in that water? You couldn't see an inch into it for the silt.

We came upon some people on a bank. Our captain pulled to them and stopped. Eight people boarded with a barrel of chicha wrapped in a black trash bag. They wore hesitant smiles. It was probably not every day that white folks rode the river. There was a little girl of maybe two years with them. She kept herself glued to the side of the boat so that she could angle her head back and stare at us. She was one I was sure hadn't seen a white person. I was back in the child's pure and innocent judgment and curiosity. She didn't look scared. Instead, it appeared as if she was piecing together what she was looking at.

Imagine being given ten seconds to look at an alien. How many of those seconds would you waste by looking away? Our very human nature is that we're so curious we must come to a conclusion. "Details! We need more details! And more time!" we'd shout. This toddler was going to use her entire boat ride to figure us out. That was okay with me.

We dropped them off a while later. It had been a quiet ride. I was exploring my thoughts rather deeply, thinking of how this ride down the river was like watching the evolution of the human shelter. At Jose's, ninety percent of the building materials for his structures were pulled directly from nature. All were unaltered no more than their placement using Shuar techniques. Getting downriver, we'd see thatched-roof huts increasingly mixed with dimensional-lumber structures. Another hour further, and the huts were gone. Another half hour downriver, and I noticed some cement blocks being used. And later, there was a modern house respective of its region. The relationship of distance from the road equaled the complexity of the dwellings.

The word *Vietnam* kept coming to mind too. The river and the jungle combined to fulfill an image of Vietnam I had somehow conjured. It probably came from pop culture. I certainly had never been to Vietnam. Here, the terrain was of a look that I hadn't even remotely associated with Ecuador. That mental territory was owned by beautiful mountains. This was one of those moments in travel where, if I was blindfolded and placed there, then allowed a look around and asked where I was, I would've quickly said, "Vietnam."

The ride ended at a dock in a primitive-looking village. One of its ten buildings served as a restaurant. A few were homes. We believed this to be Puerto Morona, or near Puerto Morona. To this day, that's still just a guess. In the complete absence of signage, Celine and I could not know where we were or where we were supposed to be to meet the taxi. She went off for answers, as her Spanish was far better than mine. She was also much more likely to engage others. I held watch over our two trash bags' worth of stuff and waved at people.

After ten minutes, I got bored, grabbed our things, and went looking for her. She had found a makeshift general store among the structures. I found her talking to a forty-something man behind the counter. He was as friendly looking as they come. But Celine's Swissness was running loose. I walked up to discover there was a problem. This time, she was in the right.

Celine had purchased something and had laid her prescription glasses down on the counter. In the tiny moment of distraction, while she dug for her money in her bag, the man swiftly took her glasses. Their value was 130 Euros. By the time I got there, she had already hashed it out that there was no other place they could be because she just had them. The guy was lying to her with a smile on his face. He knew there was nothing she could do about it. Now here's where I could have been brave or smart.

I didn't like that my travel partner was just taken advantage of. Even more, I didn't like our odds if I shook him down. He looked to be of no real physical threat. However, since the moment we stepped off the canoe, I started counting machetes. There weren't but a dozen or so men in this tiny village. But all of them had machetes. I had nothing but sunburn on my side, so the move to make was to eat this one and get the heck out of there with our necks.

Celine wouldn't have it. She protested until it began to attract attention to the man's open-air store counter. Surprisingly, a young fella, taller than me, came over to see what was going on. He was the only guy without a machete. His interest was that he was a taxi driver. He saw us as an opportunity for business. Celine took this as a chance to have him negotiate with the other guy for her glasses. He wouldn't. I knew it right away. She couldn't see it in his eyes that he didn't give a shit if she lost her glasses. Moreover, he certainly knew we were outnumbered.

For the flaws Celine perceived in me the night before, I was way ahead of her in street smarts. Growing up in West Virginian trailer parks will teach you a thing or two. There was no way the taxi driver would take the side of a strange foreigner over someone he knew. And, in no way would he snitch. I knew that he knew the clerk had the glasses. Their body language, and their shared grins, was as easy to read as the ABCs. In much of West Virginia, outsiders are disliked just for being outsiders. I had faced that dislike myself when it was directed at me by West Virginians who didn't know I was a native. Here, we were more off the grid than anywhere in my state. These men had that same deep, country dislike of outsiders that I had come to know from my home.

In a moment of clarity, Celine gave in and let the taxi driver take us to the next town. One thing we did gather from the clerk, as well as the taxi driver, was that the canoe captain took us four kilometers too far downriver. It's possible that we were on the border of Peru or had crossed into Peru unknowingly. We never could tell.

The canoe captain was gone by then. We got in the taxi and started back upstream. Celine's fire began burning once more. She just couldn't let it go. She demanded the driver stop the car. His unwillingness to help her negotiate for her glasses made her boil by his eagerness in taking our business.

We got out of the car and took our things from the trunk. The taxi driver was pissed off over this. He was becoming sarcastic. The situation was degrading. Then he sent Celine to her outer limits of disgust when he finished the soda he was drinking and threw the plastic bottle to the roadside.

I found that you don't do that in front of a Swiss woman and expect silence. Celine lit into him over his littering as if she was totally ignorant of the cultural differences between the Swiss and the rest of the world. To me, she broke a cardinal rule of travel. She projected her values upon a man who didn't know her from a pothole. All the while, she was engulfed in his culture and in his country. I remained calm. I had to be rational before I found myself as chopped-up fish bait. I loved my family too much to lose my life over a pair of glasses and a plastic bottle. I plainly wasn't offended.

Shit, I grew up on country roads where trash dumps

were commonplace. I'm not saying it was right. I'm just saying the only thing that me and Celine had in common was white skin. Looking around, men with machetes weren't out of sight as we'd barely left the village. And now, we had nearly everyone's attention. Her voice just wasn't helping.

The resolution was that we'd walk upstream to the next town. It was early enough in the day to have the light to do so. So, off we went. A half hour later, we almost laughed at how crazy that was and how we found ourselves randomly walking down a road in the jungle. The sun was bright. The air was crisp and clean, and the temperature was perfect. Radical-looking flowers lined the road. We'd have missed seeing them otherwise. It wasn't all bad.

We heard a horn from behind. An old man stopped in a white truck. He'd noticed all the commotion and offered us a ride. His eyes were forgiving. Celine and I jumped in the back with our things. The adventure took on yet another brief phase as we drove off.

The next village would've been no more than a couple-hour walk, but it was a quick drive. We waited there for our ride to come with a high amount of uncertainty. We still didn't know if we were in the right place. But as fate would have it, a young taxi driver named Barnaby spotted us an hour later. He ushered us into his car. There was a three-hour drive to get back to Macas.

I took this as a chance for a nap, as I was operating on about two hours of sleep. I leaned the front seat back and dozed off quickly. In but a handful of miles, a commotion woke me after the car came to a stop. Young men standing in the road with a rope strung across. As I opened my eyes, a young man dressed in a pink dress and wearing lipstick stuck his head in the passenger window directly above me. He demanded money. I had just come out of a dead-to-the-world snooze. *What the hell is going on?*

We learned from Barnaby that Ecuador has a New Year's tradition of teenage boys dressing as girls and doing this exact thing. It wasn't looked upon as convenient by anyone. But it was thought of as a good time. Sometimes, the boys would get paid. Sometimes not. To be awakened so bizarrely by that young man had me thinking that I may have still been in a dream. It was incredibly weird. On our way to Macas, we were stopped by cross-dressing youths several more times.

That encounter was enough to stir me to complete wakefulness. I thought, *I've seen it all now.* That was until Barnaby claimed to be too tired to drive for fear of falling asleep at the wheel. He offered us the chance to drive. Celine eagerly volunteered as she was most rested. Barnaby took the rear seat, sitting in the middle. He fell asleep as we navigated back to Macas in the dark. It was the last day of December 2016.

Baños and the Bus

Beginning a new year and a new journey is a cause for celebration. I'd soon be leaving Macas, but not before a little New Year's fun. The town was in full showcase mode for the holiday. Celine, Hanna, and I walked to the town center to experience how Ecuadorians bring in the new year. The atmosphere was theatrical. A stage had been set up. We arrived to actors performing in some sort of play. Due to the language barrier, the plot was beyond my understanding. But body language came through, again, to help me along.

A man dressed as an elderly cripple played the part of a slickster. His role was one of acting helpless when he engaged with the other actors. When they'd look away, he became alive, capable, and ready. The other characters would see him and show him pity. Then they'd turn, and he'd dance or pull a sly move. The dialogue had the crowd roaring. His voice was gravely and animated. His body language was universal.

I focused on what I could understand. I could understand the families who came out to watch. I could understand that none of them were engaged with their digital screens. And I could understand that free, live performances in town centers are as engaging as they were in the days of Shakespeare.

I roamed away from my two acquaintances to have a closer look at the performance. Two thoroughly drunk men approached me asking for a dollar, saying, "¿Un dolar?" They asked repeatedly, and I declined repeatedly. I wasn't carrying any money. The alcohol allowed them selective hearing. They didn't believe me. Instead, they took great pleasure in engaging with me. I was some sort of novelty seen through their beer goggles.

It was a harmless interaction. It was the only engagement by Ecuadorians, clearly directed toward me, that had the potential to swing in a negative direction during the entire three months in Ecuador. That is if they became upset that I didn't give them money. They were drunk enough that I couldn't predict how they'd take the news of no handouts. The fella who flipped me the bird, in Loja, left no potential for engagement as he was the passenger of a car that was driving away. Celine's actions in the Amazon were her own, and the resulting responses were directed at her. Albeit, the consequences could have been negative for both of us.

I wholeheartedly enjoyed the New Year's celebration. My time in Macas had been relatively smooth. It was fulfilling, and I loved being engulfed by the family. There wasn't a second felt of being unwelcome by Lucia. My Spanish took a great stride in those couple weeks. That's not to say that I knew Spanish. It was more like I doubled and retained my vocabulary. And I had picked up on some phrases and nuances in the use of the language. I became a believer in total immersion for learning a second language. Despite the moments of feeling foolish, it was coming along.

The time in Macas had shown such rich novelty. Like seeing the giant stems of seventy-plus bananas, at the market, for $1.50. Or, watching young teens pedal three-wheeled carts full of vegetables and earning their own living. There was a moment when Josie and I walked to Macas's motorcycle shop. There, I tried talking bikes with a fella in Spanish. Our shared appreciation of riding superseded the spotty conversation. Standard Ecuadorian life had been experienced through my eyes. But I couldn't stay in Macas. We moved on to my next phase of foreign life, Lucia-style.

On January 6, 2017, my journey back to Vilcabamba began with a third nighttime kidnapping. This was by far the earliest Lucia woke me. It was 12:30 a.m. This time, I had a grasp on where we were going, but I had missed the part where we'd get two hours of sleep before leaving. We were headed to a town whose name translates to English cleanly as bathrooms—Baños, Ecuador. Formally and less commonly used, Baños de Agua Santa is the town's actual name. It translates to Holy Water Baths. And in far less clean fashion, Lucia and her sisters would giggle when they'd joke that the town of Baños can also translate to Toilets.

Vilcabamba sat strongly southwest of us. Baños was a little northwest of Macas—about five hours by bus. In the dark of night, I knew to just follow the lead of each long, 'Miiike' that came from Lucia. We walked a few blocks to the bus terminal. Fortunately, there was time to nap on the ride.

We stepped off the bus at seven a.m. I noted right away that Baños was special. Though it was drizzling, dense fog lingered to create white skirts on Baños's steep surrounding mountains. We were in the low portion of a heavenly valley. To look through the fog, there was an air of being in a mystical land. Or rather, a feeling of enchantment where you know the residents know they live somewhere special.

Certain American towns have this quality I'd call *extra*. I've felt it in Helen, Georgia; Sedona, Arizona; Florida's Key West, and in many of California's Sierra Nevada mountain towns. I've experienced it in the Pacific Northwest's coastal villages and Colorado's ski towns. I'd acknowledge this as a quality of my hometown of Harpers Ferry, West Virginia. These places are phenomenally beautiful and demand the imagination be sparked.

Baños's mountains were the steepest I had encountered in Ecuador. They weren't radically different from Vilcabamba's, but they were greener, wetter, and more heavily vegetated. A fantastic waterfall skipped its way down one of them. Left and right, it traveled. It was out of sight. Then, it moved back in and back out. We could make out its spectacular overall height and its frantic path down the mountain from our long-distance view.

Lucia knew the itinerary. I didn't, and it was fine with me. Between us, there was simply no asking, "What would you like to do," followed by several answers of activities and discussion upon which to choose. In the absence of shared language, it was like constantly operating at seventy percent human capacity.

She found a tour outfitter. We boarded a large, heavy-duty truck. Bench seats had been installed in the rear. The truck was painted with vibrant colors. Latin, dance music pumped from the speakers like a nightclub. At thirty-five years old, it was a little too early in the morning to be cranking so loud. But we weren't the norm on the truck. We were surrounded by young tourists. They didn't mind. We were headed somewhere in style. Traveling with Lucia was always a surprise.

She had arranged that we go to a somewhat world-famous treehouse named Casa de Arbol. For a treehouse, there wasn't much to remark about. Its construction style was of the quality of a treehouse built by a dad, in his spare time, in the back yard. What made the treehouse stand alone was its location and attached swings. On either side were cantilevered timbers anchoring the rope for the swings. The positioning was just so that you'd launch off of a raised platform to swing unnervingly high over the mountainside. The ropes were long enough to send you into the wild and free air. At full swing, a person could be twenty-five feet off the ground. I felt completely detached from the Earth. The fog was so thick that you could barely make out the ground below. That, and the steep mountainside, made for a feeling of danger at full extension. As any rational adult, I simply hoped the ropes would hold. They called this the swing at the end of the world.

On a clear day, a brilliant view accompanied the swing. Slightly off to the left, and close enough to be right in your face, was the 16,480' Tungurahua Volcano. I sensed that Lucia hoped we could see it. Though, the fog had gotten the best of us. Tungurahua's base was only five miles from that swing. While in town earlier, I'd noticed a warning sign that read, "Volcano territory." At that time, I hadn't a clue we were so close. Nor was Tungurahua a sleeping giant. Its last eruptive episode had been as close as ten months before my visit. What I missed, for the fog, was seeing a steady plum of ash and its white cap. Tungurahua's elevation is above the snowline by a couple hundred feet.

The party truck shuttled us back to town. On the way, evidence of what made Baños beautiful was displaced from a mountainside. Our truck avoided a small landslide by being late to it by mere minutes. Mud had made it all the way across the road while trees and bushes completely covered one of the driving lanes. There was just enough room for us to maneuver around on the shoulder.

I reflected on places that I'd felt were stunningly beautiful. Wild and rapid erosion was a factor in all of them. Baños couldn't have been so sheer and beautiful without the formation of the Andes and their subsequent erosion. I once noted a sign on Highway 1 in coastal California that read, "Constantly Moving

Ground." Coastal California is one of Earth's most beautiful places. I was struck once more by a now-familiar feeling as we moved about Baños. Its terrain, too, innately felt like California.

I was in an exceptionally good mood as Lucia and I took off on foot to somewhere else. The town was showing us similar home construction styles as the rest of Ecuador. Concrete and block heavily dominated the process. One could notice an unorthodox nature to building homes in countries lacking zoning ordinances. Baños was another perfect example of this.

There were your nicely finished homes, and there were works in progress. What I enjoyed was that each home or business was a close reflection of its owner's vision. They didn't have to appease their neighbors. These houses looked like somewhat creative free-for-alls. One of Baños's homes looked straight-up like a castle—a handmade castle. The US is plagued by cookie-cutter designs and vast swaths of McMansions. Other than their size, they'd never been attractive enough to fetch my glances. In much of Ecuador, you'd not be surprised to find an element of creativity in nearly every home, from color to shape. I think the Andes birthed this creativity. Baños was comfortable to my traveling eyes.

My good mood skyrocketed as we came to a bridge over a slot canyon. I approached in full readiness to look down. Then I was blown away! A twenty-foot-wide, muddy river raged down below. It churned and bubbled, flowing ferociously through the canyon. Butterflies welled up inside, knowing that, should the handrail break, I'd meet my maker. The walls of the canyon were vertical from the river to the top. They were so steep that, for most of the canyon's length, even plants couldn't take hold.

We walked around a bend and to the opposite bank of the river. From this vantage, we could see where a broad and swift river met a near dead end at the mouth of the canyon. Nature had forced a hundred feet of white water to submit to twenty feet of canyon. This created an enormous natural power washer flow.

If that wasn't enough, there was an outfitter who'd let me zipline over it. Two things really pull at my heart—pizza and ziplines. With all of the good vibes flowing from the river and the town, I really wanted to try it. *The price has to be too much,* I thought. The outfitter quoted five dollars. I could have jumped for joy.

I was loaded into a green metal basket and taken, by cable, across the river at the height of the zipline. My guess was eighty feet. On the launch bank of the river, there wasn't much more than a platform. I was helped into a harness before I took off. This zipline was faster and longer than any I'd been on before. I flew for some 300 feet. Ziplines are ziplines. We know that risk equals reward. It was every bit as fun or terrifying as you care to imagine, though, for me, it was pure fun.

Baños was a delight, but on we went. We weren't headed back to Macas. Rather, I was taking the long route back to Vilcabamba. There would be a series of stops and overnights to get there. I was in Lucia's wake and eager to experience more. Our bus tickets said we were headed to a place called Guayaquil—Ecuador's largest city.

From Baños, the bus glided nicely through roads that otherwise looked too tight. Here, in the mountains of the Tungurahua Province, the hills rose and fell like the abrupt folds in a blanket. Perhaps due to more rainfall, agriculture had quite the vertical foothold here. Whereas in Kansas, you might look out of a vehicle and see one field while watching it disappear into the horizon. Here, you could see an entire mountainside of fields manipulated into rectangles, squares, and trapezoids. It was as if God had given grandma an airplane-sized needle, and she used it to sew a mountain-sized quilt. These quilts had been sewn with all of the greens of nature. Some were blazing greens. Some were army greens. Each mountain quilted in those greens was rich with crops and heavenly to the eye.

We turned southwest to Riobamba for a bus transfer. This was an unexpected stop in a town I had hoped to pass through while in Ecuador. Riobamba is in the Chimborazo Province. The name undoubtedly came from the Chimborazo Volcano that lays in the far northwest of the province. There were few things I learned about Ecuador before arriving. One was of the 20,564-foot Chimborazo Volcano. It's Ecuador's highest peak. It's one degree south of the equator. And it's most famously known for its summit being the furthest terrestrial point away from the center of the Earth.

If you imagine Earth not being perfectly round, but instead picture it contorted so that it's thicker at the equator than it is from north to south, you'd have Earth's actual shape in mind. The shape is kind of like giant hands had applied pressure to the north and south poles in a failed effort to flatten the planet.

This feature of our planet is called the equatorial bulge. It's enough to scramble the mind when we find out that Chimborazo pokes further into space than Mt. Everest—even with Everest's 8,465-foot advantage. The Earth is large enough to have the equatorial bulge yet still look near perfectly round. Thinking of such things contorts my brain.

Through the bus window, Chimborazo's glory and mass showed from its base to about 1000 feet. Higher than that, the volcano was utterly lost in the clouds. Chimborazo is one of those things that makes it worth it to revisit Ecuador. One day, I'd like to engrave the sight of the giant into my memory for nothing more than experience.

The land southwest of Riobamba kept a strong agricultural look. Now, the giant folds of the Tungurahua Province were gone and replaced by gently rolling, green pastures and fields. There wasn't a hint of this area not feeling peaceful. We were cruising at an elevation of eight to nine thousand feet. The thought of farmers having really good, wholesome existences here owned my mind. The evening glow enhanced their crops to, at times, make the rolling hills look unnatural or backlit as a television would be. I was happy to be gliding comfortably in a bus through this wonderland.

Just before evening, a young man boarded the bus. He remained standing at the front and dug a flute out of his pack. He was Ecuadorian. His motivation was to earn some money. Lucia and I were sitting about four rows back. He began playing somewhat wispy folk tunes with his flute. They sounded like memories that had come to life. In Lucia, I sensed she was enjoying this tremendously. I'm sure she would've loved to tell me the name of the tunes or the story behind them. The pride was so heavy with her. The young man was playing the sound of Ecuador.

I could relate in that West Virginia has its own sound. Thanks to John Denver's *Country Roads*, every time I'm away from home and hear it, I have to fight off a frog in my throat. Hearing "West Virginia, mountain mama" strums my soul chord. It's all the same for people who are proud of where they're from. I met no one prouder of her Ecuador than Lucia.

The young man earned some change. I gave him a dollar of my own. He exited the bus after four tunes worth of stops. We were facing nighttime shortly after. Guayaquil wasn't far off now. I sure wished I could still see the land as the outside world fell to darkness.

Guayaquil and the Girls
and the Beach and the Birds

Big cities aren't a representation of my nature. I've lived an hour and a half from Washington, D.C. my whole life. Beyond going there for work, I've done all that I could to not visit the place. Outside of the Smithsonian, and the chance for diverse food, I really don't enjoy anything about my nation's capital. The traffic is horrible. If the traffic light turns green, and you're late to start driving by a millisecond, the asshole behind you will blow their horn. The people certainly haven't been welcoming or friendly to me. In D.C., eye contact is usually matched with a cold glare, if you're lucky enough to make eye contact at all.

My nation's capital is like a lost soul who can't see that materialism never brings happiness. That's my worthless opinion on big cities born from five years working in and around Washington's metro region. Now, with Lucia, I had just arrived in another big city. I wondered what was in store as caution grew inside.

First, we had to meet Blanca. Though she was in Macas for the holidays, Guayaquil was her home. We met her at the bus terminal and taxied to her neighborhood. Traveling at night, I couldn't tell if I was in a city in my country or theirs. At a certain point, city size invites similar features. There are giant buildings, lots of traffic, people milling about, lights, outlandish energy consumption, parks, statues, and countless businesses. Those are basic city features to a country boy. If I were only going to have two nights in Guayaquil, I'd have to pay attention to the small things to stand a chance of knowing anything about the place. A caveat to that is that there's no way to know a big city in just two nights.

Guayaquil was alive with activity. The first thing that set Guayaquil apart from my experience in the United States, and in Ecuador, were the hordes of powered rickshaws or motorcycle taxis. I'm really not sure how they were locally described. Being nighttime, I noticed parking lots with young men sitting in, and standing beside, their machines. No expense seemed to be spared in jazzing up their rides. They were colorfully painted and brightly lit. The scene reminded me of parking lots at home on Friday nights where the kids would gather to show off their cars. The difference being these fellas were working. I imagined that the more novel the rickshaw, the more business it pulled.

That was it for making it to Blanca's house. I noticed nothing else out of the ordinary. However, at Blanca's, I was smacked in the face with a realization of where I was in the world. Blanca lived on a paved street in a two-story townhome. Access to her street came from unlocking a tall, heavy gate. On top of that gate was the same wicked razor wire that prisons use. If I didn't think, *Do I really want to be here?* I'd be lying. *Is this really what it takes to keep ownership of your stuff and sleep safely at night in Guayaquil? Wow! This is wild!* Blanca was of the gentlest of nature, surviving in a city requiring this of its residents. I didn't let the girls know this alarmed me. Once inside, I felt safer.

We didn't stay there long, though. I was with Lucia. Predictably, plans morphed, and she was ready to show me Guayaquil. We'd leave and meet their sister Linda and Linda's son Miguel. Another ride across town showed me a city alive with people enjoying the nightlife. Street performers, especially musicians, were plentiful. Folks stood watching, looking alert and awake. They bathed in the abundant energy of the enormous city.

We met Linda at a park and took off on foot. The girls expressed that I would be fine as we walked around together, but they insisted that I was not to walk around alone. We headed for Santa Ana Hill. It seemed, to me, to be the city center. Wildly colored homes were the flavor of the hill. Blues and oranges stood out the most. In the daytime, it must have looked even more festive given those colors. I followed, taking in the sights and keeping my head on a swivel. I was focused on being a wise traveler. Pickpocketing was on my mind. *Why wouldn't the women let me explore on my own if there was nothing to worry about?* Yet, I didn't care to go alone after spotting the razor wire.

At the base of Santa Ana Hill, we began to climb numbered stairs. There was stair number one, then two, then three, and on it went. On either side of us were two-story buildings hosting restaurants and nightclubs. Music pumped here. We were ascending a slot canyon of good-times energy. We were halfway at step 222. I had already internalized how I would've loved to party here in my twenties. Back then, I'd huck myself into most any situation without regard to safety. I lived reckless and wild on the weekends. This street was a Bourbon Street with steps. If only I could have partied there.

At step 444, we reached the top. Seeing Guayaquil, as a bird sees it, showed me a city sprawled far to the night's horizon. Pale, yellow lights highlighted the smaller building locations below. The color of the lights was an unsurprising feature of the city. In the United States, we've gone to lighting that glows more whitish. Throughout Ecuador, and in my travels along the Mexican border, I've seen that something is different with the outside lighting in other countries. I've noticed this stark difference most clearly on Interstate 10 in El Paso, Texas. In El Paso, everything is more crisply lit. Looking over the border at Juarez, Mexico, shows a city of duller-glowing lights.

Santa Ana Hill gave Guayaquil a San Francisco feel. A sixty-foot lighthouse stood tall and was open for touring. We went up to the lookout deck. The view was much the same. A few skyscrapers poked into the night sky. I expected a greater number of them. An antique of a chapel sat at the opposite end of Santa Ana Hill. The ground lights illuminating its front gave it an air of mystery in the night. Perhaps it was the exercise from the steps, but I was feeling pretty happy to be exploring and less worried as a traveler.

We descended the stairs back into the party zone. I still held the feeling of wanting to get loose there. Internally, I knew it wasn't going to happen. Linda's son Miguel accompanied me down the stairs, pointing out things to notice and telling me about Guayaquil. In his fifteen years, he'd developed an operable understanding of English. I took my camera out to record this area as we walked.

We passed a twenty-something man out for an evening. He looked sharp with a nice shirt on and wearing dark sunglasses, despite being night. He noticed me and said, in English, "My friend. Where are you from?" I replied, "Here." He laughed and said, "Okay, my friend. Welcome to Guayaquil." He definitely knew better.

And just like that, I was back in defense mode. I suppose I asked for the attention by holding my camera high to film. Miguel earnestly said I shouldn't have lied to the guy. He was offended that I had lied. This caught me off guard. The context in which I was operating was that, under no circumstances would I put myself in danger. I figured it would be stupid to yell a response, especially over the loud music, that I'm from the United States. I hadn't forgotten that I wasn't allowed to explore on my own or that Blanca's house was guarded by razor wire. Miguel certainly had a better feel for Guayaquil and probably recognized I wasn't in danger. Our differing contexts were based on radically different lives lived.

I wasn't sure if Miguel had experienced American media or knew its conditioning upon us. It's practically protocol to think the world is out to get us for our perceived individual wealth. My five previous years living slightly above the level of a drifter meant that I was anything but a wealthy American. I was also guilty of paying too close attention to stories of Americans traveling abroad and getting their heads lopped off. It only took one decapitation for me to conclude that I'd rather not experience that.

Miguel projected a different vibe toward me afterward. I didn't want that to be the case. We were both partially correct in how we interpreted the situation. These are lessons we learn as we travel. I don't take pride in lying, but I weigh the options. That man could have phoned his buddies and said, "An American is heading down the steps holding a camera. Take it." Or, "Take him!" That's why I lied. Miguel saw it as disrespecting a local. Who's to say what would've happened?

In the years that have passed, I've been haunted by the internal need to settle what bothered me about my lie. What was there to learn? To have that moment again, I would've replied with something vague but dead honest like, "I'm from the banks of the Shenandoah River." Or: "Harper's Ferry." These answers would not immediately expose my citizenship. And my conscience wouldn't remind me of the chink in my character. Maybe Miguel wouldn't have been offended. But I still wouldn't have included "The United States." Once you've been robbed, you can't go back to the naivety once held. In 2011, I was robbed at gunpoint in New Orleans. Miguel didn't know that. It's all about the context.

Our group headed back to Blanca's house for dinner. Again, we went through the gate and right back out. I understood we were going to a restaurant. We were on foot, moving through the residential streets near Blanca's. A man was outside of a house grilling. There were a couple of tables on the sidewalk, and he was accompanied by a woman I believed was his wife. This was their home, and they were serving food for profit as if it was a restaurant. We sat outside their front door and ate a traditional Ecuadorian home-cooked meal. I had rice and grilled chicken.

The girls engaged in conversation. I sat there picking up snippets of what was being said. Largely, I was lost, but my Spanish was getting better after a few weeks of mostly speaking Spanish. Those soft yellow streetlights illuminated the surroundings. A slight mist added to how much air space those lights affected. The visual ceiling was low enough not to see stars in the sky. The misty ambiance was one of privacy, despite us sitting on a sidewalk. For a big city, this was a quiet neighborhood. I absolutely loved that the man could sell food right out of his doorway. I loved how he could provide for his neighbors and bring his community together. Regulation is such a thing as to stifle so many of us would-be American entrepreneurs. After dinner, we walked back to Blanca's. And again, the razor wire caught my eye.

Blanca prepared a room for me upstairs. It was every bit of eighty-five degrees up there. Ecuador had shown me no high temperatures to this point. I'd been living in the mountains for a month. And the short time in the jungle just wasn't that hot. Now, we were a stone's throw from the Pacific and nearly at sea level. Guayaquil was hot and humid. It was what I thought the whole equatorial region would be. Still, I managed some sleep in the high temperature with the help of a fan.

In the morning, I met the girls downstairs. They were stirring and eager not to let an opportunity to travel be wasted. Linda agreed to shuttle us for the day. We took off in her car to who knows where for who knew how long. The door of surprises had swung open again.

Leaving Guayaquil, we went directly west toward the coast. The drive took on a look of East Los Angeles with similar-looking hills and commercial interests. This area was somewhat drier than the ride into Guayaquil. Markedly, the biggest difference between here and Southern California was the home construction and the model of cars on the road.

An hour in, and the terrain had changed drastically. I didn't see it coming. Linda was cruising along. All of us were happy and content. We pulled the car over to pee one time. *This land is looking awfully dry to be so close to the coast.* Things were becoming more brown than green. We hopped back in and continued on. In no time, we might as well have been somewhere in Arizona. The landscape matched full-blown, wild west desert. *Where in the hell did this come from?*

Sand and brown, and more sand and brown was about all there was. Any structures in this stretch were beaten and weathered. I sat in quiet amazement, wanting to ask a thousand questions about how we morphed from fertile to desert so quickly. My answer came much later, during research, that the area was known as Ecuadorian dry forests. Google Earth shows the area as mostly green. The dry forest is but a sliver of brown seen from satellite. As fast as we entered it, it seemed we were out of it. The cause of this drastic regional change is said to be deforestation and unsustainable agriculture. One percent of the original forest remains. Many endemic species that dwell here are critically at risk of extinction. In the moment, I saw the area as a tiny desert and another trick expressed by the land in Ecuador. I didn't know better.

Our course was still west. All had not returned fully to moist and green when we stopped in Puerto del Morro. A dryness lingered here, too. Puerto del Morro is part of an estuary where the Guayas River drains into the Gulf of Guayaquil. Puerto del Morro was a somewhat rough-looking village. A few restaurants had been kept nice for the sake of tourism. After staying in Vilcabamba and visiting Macas, Baños, Loja, and even Guayaquil, I was seeing my first rough-looking towns. Resources just seemed scarcer, as they naturally do in dry climates. I imagined us as being in one of those places that probably had more stray cats than usual. That was the vibe.

I wondered why we had stopped there. I thought we were going to the Pacific. Traveling with these women, I was no different than a mannequin with working legs. I'd keep my mouth shut and walk brainlessly to wherever they needed me to be. Lucia was my hero by now. I trusted there was a reason we were in Puerto del Morro. And, by golly, there was. Lucia wanted us to go on a boat ride. She was so full of life.

A 200-foot-wide stretch of river made for one of

Puerto del Morro's town borders. I noticed a concrete slide where sewage was seeping from town into the river. It was another one of those moments that grabs you and shakes the reality into your presence. But this was how they did it, so who was I to judge? I could only observe and reflect. A couple touring outfitter's boats sat docked at the water's edge. We picked a boat with bench seats and a roof. A young female accompanied us as a guide. We set off toward bigger water.

The banks here were flanked by mangroves growing as thick as the land would allow. The further we glided, the wider the open water. Being so close to the Pacific, these were essential shelter lands ready to take a punch from ocean storms. When the boat reached open water, we were cruising pretty fast toward an opposite shore. As with anywhere you travel, you can find something that looks like it's similar to a place you've been. This looked like the Chesapeake Bay to me. This part of the estuary was eight miles wide.

Evidence lingered in the shallow areas of old mangrove forests. Trunks poked out of the water, rising four and five feet high as eerie wooden skeletons. This was a reminder that I hadn't grown out of an apprehension of deep or unfamiliar water. I kept it close in mind that it would be unfortunate to sink the boat by running into an unseen stump below the surface. The last thing I wanted was a four-mile swim in unfamiliar saltwater.

Several minutes at wide-open speed got us to the opposite bank. The attraction here was no less surprising than any that had come before. We were surrounded by commercial fishing boats. Some were a mere sixty feet long. Some were twice that. Rusty and battered steel hulls and chipped paint made for vessels with a thousand fishing stories. Some were named Diego, Nikolay, Barbara, and even Virgin del Rosario. These crafts had pulleys and thick, sturdy cables ready for hoisting in whatever the ocean provided.

For me, the real show was the thousands of frigatebirds and hundreds of pelicans that so rudely smothered the fisherman. If there was an overhead cable, an opportunistic sea bird was perched on it, just waiting for one of the fishermen to look away. The sky was littered with wings. The men paid no attention and focused on the task. These were hard-looking fishermen. As rugged as their boats were, they carried faces to match. These were the type of guys you see bearded and battling the Bering Sea in Alaska on those fishing shows. But they were Ecuadorian, and beards were rare. Many had their sons with them. Some looked as young as fourteen.

One young teenager pulled a sixteen-foot jon boat up to an offshore fishing vessel. The moment he stopped, a pelican landed on the stern of his boat. In the distance, a wharf—packed heavily with fishing boats—sat between us and a fishing village. The village was as beaten looking as the boats. Whereas many Ecuadorian towns had homes of concrete and block, this was the same. The difference was that, here, most were left unpainted and gray. This took the pop out of them. The village looked like less of a happy place to live.

I certainly enjoyed seeing this authentic side of Ecuadorian life. Even if I was a tourist on a boat, the fishermen were not a prop to entertain me. They had families to feed and bills to pay. As a blue-collar man, I appreciated all of this greatly. We powered away from there into deeper waters. Two dolphins paralleled us when we were a quarter-mile offshore. No doubt they knew that the catch had come in. The fish were the foundation to what was needed by the mouths of so many. Man, and animal couldn't live without them here.

Two islands were in the center of the estuary. They were Isla Manglecita Grande and Isla Manglecita Chico. We were headed right for them. Each was a mile and a half in length and far less wide. As we drew closer, the sky took on a look of clouds made of birds. Everything about the presence of this many birds spelled swarm. These two islands were nesting grounds for frigatebirds. There were many times more birds here than there were at the fishing boats.

We docked at Isla Manglecito Grande. The tour guide explained to us that these islands were protected from development for the sake of the birds. A nature trail had been made to explore the island. I followed the girls along it. Very quickly, I realized this island had but few ingredients. There were the mangrove trees. There was mud and sand. And there was more bird poop than you could shake a stick at. If ever there was a place to heed the old warning, 'Don't look up with your mouth open,' this was that exact place. Thousands of frigatebirds circled above, all with their jet-fighter straight wings and rather large sizes. There was enough caca looming over us to fertilize Nebraska.

If there were a thousand birds in the air, there were three thousand in the branches. Their presence spawned a fertile ecosystem for other critters. The cacarich mud made for the homes of bright, red and blue, and rather hilarious-looking land crabs. I'll take nothing away from how pretty they actually were. They stood out in their environment like they were cartoons. We'd pass by, and they'd send their brilliant white claws skyward ready for war. Or they'd scurry into their holes. At three inches, their threat wasn't of any concern.

We did a lap around the island without being shit on. I was once shit on as a boy when I was shoveling in a field. They say it's good luck. If that's the case, this was the island of good luck. And I wasn't shit on. So, what's that say? I still thought it was a fine experience. I felt so grateful to Lucia, Blanca, and Linda for having me along.

The ride wasn't over. We had a bit of ground to cover to the west. The mighty Pacific was eight miles away. In the estuary, we weren't quite close enough to glimpse it. I wondered how similar it would look here compared to the only other time I saw the Pacific in California. Linda drove us there.

We picked a spot at a park, beachside. The park was of equal quality to any park in the coastal United States, with nice restrooms and a paved parking lot. The girls got in their swimsuits, and I threw some shorts on. Against the ocean, there was a breeze just cool enough to overpower the sunshine. Blanca and I took to the water for a swim. Here, the water of the Pacific was living up to its definition: peaceful in character or intent. Against the beach sand, there were no waves. It laid almost as flat as a pond. I didn't know this as a possibility of an ocean.

California's Pacific shore is aggressive with waves. Its water is cold and deep. Much of Ecuador had reminded me of California, but this spot gave an Eastern U.S. vibe. We were hours outside Ecuador's mountains. The terrain against the Pacific was nearly flat here. The water was shallow for a great distance from the shore. It was warm enough to be easily comfortable, too. The handfuls of sand I pulled off the bottom to investigate were nearly black. Around us, people played just like anywhere. Blanca and I were in our mid-thirties, passing colorful shells to one another as if we were ten again.

Lucia and Linda left the water early. They claimed to be cold. Given the water's temperature and the sunshine, it couldn't have felt more comfortable to me. Lucia getting cold here sparked a memory of her time in West Virginia during October. You'd think she was going to freeze to death. Blanca and I didn't keep them waiting. We transformed back to adults, took our hands out of the sand, stood up, and slowly walked to the car. Playtime was over. We were off to Guayaquil.

I felt the same amazement passing through the desert again. I noted the towns seeming rougher again. I thought of how I experienced a pinprick of the Pacific coast of Ecuador. We neither traveled north nor south along the coast. We went west to see the ocean and back. I internalized that a coastal ride would be enjoyable in the future. There was so much more to see. When I had stood on the sand of that beach, I looked west and knew the Galapagos Islands were 700 miles away. Like the missed opportunity to see the Chimborazo volcano, the awareness of the Galapagos was enough to guarantee I'd be back someday.

All in all, we had a fantastic day. To ask for anything more would've been plain selfish. To ask myself to give more would've been more like it. I say that in regards to my command of Spanish. I really wished I had given more effort to learning Spanish in school or practicing before I left home. The couple weeks at Lucia's helped tremendously. Still, in all honesty, I could get lost in communication like I could get lost in a maze. Everything about being with the girls left me wanting to be part of the conversation without being able to be. Our day had shown me reasons for a million questions, all of which were left unanswered.

In Guayaquil, we arrived back at Blanca's. Each of us had been wet, and we'd mostly dried off during the drive. My shoes got wet several times during the day. A gnarly essence accompanied them. They were like an unwanted visitor. We all knew it. In the car, I picked up on the conversation that something smelled. It was my shoes. They were fart-level stinky. Blanca wanted me to do something with them. But what?

There was some finger-pointing, matched with quick Spanish. I knew my shoes couldn't be in the house. Or could they? Did she want them off or on, outside or inside, or trashed? I didn't know. She was trying to tell me what to do with them enough to gather attention from Lucia, which doubled the Spanish words headed my way. They weren't upset that my shoes were inside—I think. Or, they could have been. I was so confused as to what to do with my shoes that I formed a weak smile. I took them off and put them in her laundry area. That room was off the side of the kitchen and exposed to the open air. The bizarre thing about this episode was I wasn't even sure if the issue they were talking to me about was regarding my shoes. I just assumed it was. I had no idea what particular stink the girls were all fired up about. Nor will I ever.

Return to Vilcabamba

Another hot Guayaquil night passed upstairs at Blanca's. I realized how spoiled I'd been at the farm in Vilcabamba. I could sleep with the window open comfortably since heat and humidity weren't problems at the high elevation.

    Morning arrived with a plan to do little more than catch the bus at nine a.m. I'd be setting sail alone on my way back to Vilcabamba. That $579 dollars, which I had brought to Ecuador, had been whittled down to just about $200. The plane trip into the Amazon was sixty-nine dollars. Bus rides had taken another sixty dollars. The bus to Vilcabamba would be nearly thirty dollars. I'd eaten several times in Vilcabamba's restaurants already. I bought a pocketknife, as well as the basics for hygiene and grooming. All required money. I was a foreigner so fortunate to have friends in Ecuador because I surely didn't have the funds for this number of experiences on my own.

I bid farewell to Lucia and Blanca at the bus terminal. There are no examples better than those two women, and their family, for being a positive representation of Ecuador. Blanca had a sense of humor with which a man could fall in love. And there were indeed more layers to Lucia than I knew. Living with her and being guided by her, showed me a woman more hospitable than any I had known before. I do wish to have a conversation with her on a return visit to Ecuador, but I'll have to earnestly learn Spanish. Both women were beautiful through and through, and I can't wait to know more about them when we can, one day, talk in depth.

As I boarded the bus, it was clear that I'd just lived the most dynamic month of my life. There had been months that were close, but none had me face my own vulnerability so consistently as the past month. The emotion from each experience afforded me unforeseen fulfillment. Had I went home right after Guayaquil, I would've been okay with that big taste of Ecuador. Yet, there were still two months before I'd leave.

I was now quite comfortable solo. The transition came quickly after Lucia and Blanca left my side. Even being alone in Guayaquil's bus terminal felt fine. I filmed openly without much concern. Then the bus sounded its horn. I boarded and looked forward to the day's travels.

To get to Vilcabamba required about ten hours and a transfer in Loja. The trip was 296 miles. That's relatively short for ten hours. Along the way, our driver took a long lunch break, and most villages required multiple stops. It was common for folks to ride the bus only to the next town. Overall, the route would have the bus stay about a dozen miles off the coast for seventy-five miles south. Then we'd turn east for the Andes.

I took a seat in the back of the bus to keep a good vantage on those who came and went. I wanted to use my camera more discreetly, too. I wasn't nervous. Sitting in the back of the bus just seemed wise at the time. The bus rolled away from the big city of Guayaquil. Though I had a good time there, I was ready to be back in the mountains. I didn't care to be reminded of the US just yet. Guayaquil had parking garages, heavy traffic, and it was humid. And when we passed a McDonald's the day before, I wished I hadn't seen it.

Notably, a theme arrived in the coastal miles outside of Guayaquil. The towns we passed weren't shaped as squares with a central church, as they had been in other parts of Ecuador. They were long strips of town paralleling the road. These were artery towns—highway towns. If not for Highway E25 running through them, they'd likely be tiny villages or ghost towns.

Many kept the look of what I'd noticed in Puerto del Morro. There was a strong usage of cinder block, left unpainted and unparged. These towns' buildings were gray with small splashes of color. Most buildings were simply unfinished-looking. That might have been the most significant difference in places like there and Vilcabamba. The homes in Vilcabamba looked more complete.

Scooters and small motorcycles were prime transportation noticed throughout the day. Safety wasn't a concern as no one wore helmets. As a motocross racer, I knew some of those folks would be facing severe road rash shortly. On motorcycles, the saying goes, "It's not if you'll fall; it's when." But such was the culture, and I was only a pair of eyes. I even saw a young man riding his motorcycle, where it was loaded high like a truck with building material. "Good luck with that," I whispered toward him.

If those towns were islands of civilization, then banana plantations were the sea of green in between. The same way the United States' Midwest is known for horizon's worth of cornfields, this region of coastal Ecuador showed me unimaginable-sized grows of banana trees. Rather, they look like trees but are classified as banana plants. I thought, *How is it possible that this many bananas are grown here, and I've never eaten one with a sticker reading, "Grown in Ecuador."* I have always looked. Simple people like me get a kick out of how far a banana can travel.

In the seventy-five miles south, I saw some banana plants fruiting and some not. The ones that did had blue protective sacks covering full stems of bananas. And a single stem may have held dozens of green bananas. I guessed the blue sacks helped fight off bugs or were there to speed up ripening.

We were cruising effortlessly through the coastal towns. The highway was flat and fast here. With little more than bananas to observe, I began noticing signs designating areas as cantóns. One sign read, "Bienvenido al Cantón Machala." (Welcome to Machala) I wondered, "Does cantón mean county?" It does not. But it's not far off.

Ecuador's cantóns are a layer of subdivision that fits between the larger provinces and are divided by the smaller parishes within. From what I was able to determine, cantóns can be just like counties. A cantón can also be a city. Cuenca, Ecuador, is both a city and a cantón. Though, defining cantóns results in some vagueness. Ecuador is divided into twenty-four provinces and 221 cantóns.

From Vilcabamba to Macas, Macas to Guayaquil, and now back to Vilcabamba, most buses would play American movies on a screen at the front of the bus. Being a Latin American country, these American movies were altered to have Spanish-speaking, voiceover actors speaking the parts of the English-speaking actors. *The Transporter,* a film starring Jason Statham, played through. The voice given him was a deep, clear, and serious Spanish voice. It was unlike Statham's raspy, whispery, and measured natural tone.

I watched Tom Hank's, *Sleepless in Seattle* play on another bus. I'd put my money on the voice for Hanks being the same one used as Jason Statham's character. I was mixed about this, knowing how different those men sound in real life. There was great hilarity hearing Tom Hanks sounding like a tough guy.

We came to another cantón. Its welcome sign read, "Bienvenido al Cantón Santa Rosa." Here, while in a traffic circle where the bus was lunged to one side, the grace of holy music vibration hit my ears. Bryan Adam's song, *Heaven,* played through the speakers—in English! The drawn-out love lyrics didn't get me. It was his native-tongued English that got me. I missed it! My God, it was honey to my ears. My wiring was momentarily complete.

For four minutes, I could effortlessly understand human language. I felt lighter. Dopamine undoubtedly surged in my brain as to reward me and say, "You need to seek out more of this. You're struggling in Spanish world." Hearing him sing, *Baby, you're all that I want*, came to me as pure comprehension. Switch the word baby with the word English, and keep the lyric; *you're all that I want*. That's how I felt!

I didn't know how much I missed it. Sure, I'd heard English from Celine and Hanna, but they had thick Swiss accents that required me to pay attention when they spoke. Bryan Adam's genuine American dictation was sent straight from above. The past couple of weeks had felt like shuffling down the sidewalk without lifting my feet. There was friction in every word heard and exchanged.

I felt a slight boost to my mood after that. Now, we were heading east toward the mountains. The ride slowed dramatically. We were back in the land of steep inclines and roads that zigzagged as sharply as Arabic letters. I was in no hurry, nor did I lack faith that we'd get there. I was happy to be back in the mountains, out of the humidity, back in the world of plentiful green and more finished-looking towns.

On one stop, a young woman boarded the bus with a tray of cut fruit. Her hustle was to sell that tray of fruit before the new people boarded and the bus took off. She had everything cut into single-bite blocks and packaged in cups. I purchased one for a dollar with a smile. The cup was primarily of grapes with chopped mango and sliced bananas.

The progression of nicer villages and more beautiful mountains continued to Catamayo, Ecuador. The sky was clear and blue now. In the strangest of ways, entering Catamayo felt like coming home. This was territory I'd been through. I landed in Catamayo one month prior on my way to Vilcabamba. My nerves were so shot then that I couldn't pay attention to the town. Now I could absorb that it was beautiful, colorful, and clean. I felt peacefulness riding the bus into Catamayo. The mountains did have a drier look to them than I remembered. Yet, they still stood impressively over Catamayo's fertile green valley. I remembered looking at that valley through the plane's window during the flight to southern Ecuador. I felt so incredibly far from home then.

One hour separated Catamayo from Loja by bus. And Loja was even more familiar territory since I celebrated Christmas there with Iliana and her family. We pulled into Loja's terminal for a transfer to the bus going to Vilcabamba. I disembarked as if I lived there. I knew the window in which to approach. I had a pocketful of Spanish words at the ready for purchasing a ticket. I even had a dime for the waiting turnstile. I wasn't worried about being pickpocketed. The people of Loja conducted themselves better than that. The absolute freaked-out Mike, from a month before, had melted away. I had some wings now. I could locomote around fairly comfortably.

As I sat on the bus to Vilcabamba, thoughts came of how silly it was of me to be such a nervous wreck. I was embarrassed by how unconfident I was in my ability to figure out the logistics of the terminal, and even more embarrassed at my lack of confidence in my ability to handle myself in a threatening situation. Confidence comes from practice and experience. One month in Ecuador had increased my confidence. Enough, anyway. Handling Loja's bus terminal smoothly felt like a lesson that needed to be learned.

 I arrived in Vilcabamba in a heavy rainstorm. It was pitch black. I needed a taxi. I knew where to get one and how to direct the man to the farm. I was traveling so well now and had grand stories I couldn't wait to share with my American friends. There were volcanoes, leaf-cutter ants, a girl who ate a worm, Mamita Building, Swiss women, Jose and the Amazon, and hot waterfalls. There was a magical adventure town named Baños, swarms of birds, the pacified Pacific, Ecuador's largest city, and a desert that came out of nowhere.

Saraguro and Cuenca

I didn't find it easy to make friends with the Ecuadorians without the help of others along the way. Largely, they minded their business, and I'm of the same nature. Iliana introduced us to her family. With her help, becoming friends with them was easy. It was the same with Lucia. The desire was in me to make a few friends on my own, but credit had to be given where it was due. Others plainly opened the door of interactions with Ecuadorians for me. Alice was the prime door opener. One afternoon in Vilcabamba, she introduced me to a humble and kind man named Angel.

    Angel came to Vilcabamba every few weeks to sell bead jewelry his family had hand-crafted. Though I'm not a wearer of jewelry, I was impressed by their ability to make designs like hummingbirds, butterflies, lizards, and funny little ears of corn. Angel was the type of man who perfectly fit into who he was, so much so that you couldn't wipe the smile off of his face. Most intriguing, though, Angel was of the Saraguro people.

They're a face of South America that had made it to my eyes a few times through the television screen. I always found their attire bizarre. They wear traditional, black top hats, shin-length, black pants, and heavy woolen shaws—some colorful. Their hair is often long and braided. They're exceptionally formal in appearance, the way the Amish are in the States.

Despite an effort to research an exact reason for their clothing choice, I couldn't find anything solid enough to deem accurate. One source said they dress formally to mourn the death of the Inca Emperor Atahualpa—the last Inca emperor. Another source claimed that black clothing is better for retaining heat in higher elevations. There are fluid opinions on these subjects that explain why they keep their hair long and braided and why both sexes wear large hats. Those hats are sometimes black, sometimes white, and sometimes both. I'm just a hillbilly without a degree, so I had to leave it alone.

Even in that limited capacity, however, I do have the wits to recognize that there's no way to mention the Saraguro without noting their clothing. Even the Amazon's Shuar people dressed closer to the modern world. The Saraguro are doing their own thing. I chose to focus on what I could understand, which was reciprocating the kindness that Angel showed me.

Alice made plans to go to Cuenca and visit her American friend, June. I was invited along. She said we'd stop in Saraguro for lunch and see Angel as well. I was excited to visit him, meet his family, and be amid folks whose tradition I couldn't comprehend. Plus, I'd arranged a little side project for him involving making a green, beaded frog for my mother. I wanted to trade him some money for it.

From Vilcabamba, Saraguro is forty-five miles north as the crow flies and sixty-nine miles by road. We took the bus for a weekend trip. By now, I'd passed through to Loja several times. Still, I hadn't been directly north to Saraguro. Spying out the windows of the bus, I came to find only minor changes to the terrain between the villages. Rolling green hills, full of pastures, and triangular mountains, were also common near Saraguro. If anything, it seemed to be slightly more of a moist environment. I'd say the greens were filled in more than Vilcabamba. We arrived in the rain, so that may have also thrown me off.

Saraguro was small. A first impression showed me that the roofs were not of the same orange terracotta tile as many of Vilcabamba's homes. Here, I noticed dark brown terracotta tiles. Maybe the buildings were older, or the roofs laden with moss, or the terracotta was formed from darker clay. That observation accompanied another. This was a town where bright paint colors were somewhat muted among the homes. Saraguro had a drab look about it. Again, the rainy day may have had something to do with it.

The central square had been slightly jazzed up with painted stone pavers. A generous use of yellow paint stood out among the pavers. Some brilliantly colored murals helped to counteract the drab ambiance. They were a welcomed mood elevator in the rain.

Before we could meet Angel, we grabbed lunch at a restaurant in the central square. Inside, two televisions were playing Donald Trump's inauguration. The news anchors spoke Spanish, and the captioning was in Spanish. I didn't need to know what they were saying. My mind was trying to wrap around whether or not what I was seeing was real. My gut had told me for months that Hillary Clinton was undoubtedly going to be our next president. I saw her as capable of nefariously using her political clout to make it happen. *How could the establishment lose?* I questioned. But I was incredibly wrong.

In a moment where the election's integrity should have been celebrated, in that it wasn't rigged after all—Clinton got more votes. Still, she succumbed to the rules relating to the Electoral College. I sat there shocked. *Is there a country called the United States where a brand-spanking-new politician is actually going to become the president? Are we seriously going to be governed by a non-establishment candidate? What in the world is going on there?* I'm not saying I thought it was a good or bad thing. I'm expressing my overall disbelief. How unbelievable that a citizen beat the corrupt Washington machine. No matter the citizen's name. I wondered, *Is this television somehow programmed to project this image?* What I was seeing felt psychedelic in nature. It seemed like the television was broadcasting some sort of propaganda. It felt like I was on a far-out trip without the drugs.

I was in shock despite being without a political affiliation. I've never wanted to tarnish my own good character by adopting a label from either giant party.

I'm way too free-spirited, and also great at tarnishing my character through sheer foolishness. No further help is needed.

With that admission, I'd not voluntarily be in a foreign land, surrounded by people radically different than myself, if I took sides or shunned differences. I do not like division. The day I was born was the day I joined the human team. United we stand; divided we fall. That's enough political crap for three books. On, I move.

An incredible level of feeling disconnected from America washed over me. Hell, I'd been speaking almost as much Spanish as English and eating insanely healthy. I was enjoying being around whole, functioning family units again. The thought that owned my mind watching that television was, *That's a country full of people who are losing their minds. They're thirsty for division.* I was happy to be disconnected from all of that drama. I had been incredibly disconnected. Though, the degree of disconnection didn't sink in until that very moment. It was the first time I felt like a foreigner to the US.

We left for Angel's after lunch. He met us in town to show us the way. Angel lived in an awfully modest home, on a hillside, on the south side of town. To reach his house, we climbed a dirt trail with steps dug into the hill. In West Virginia, we'd call this home a shack. You must understand the context of saying that. I come from the lowest level of income in West Virginia. I didn't live in a house without wheels until I was sixteen years old. Trailer parks aren't savory places in the mountain state. So, I use a descriptive term to describe his house for accuracy, rather than judgment from a perceived superiority.

It didn't matter the home. The hearts that lived there told the story. Likewise, I'd come to learn through my time in Ecuador that if you show me a shack painted bright orange, I'll show you a truly happy human living inside. Angel welcomed us in with a smile. His business was his business, while his home was where he worked. It was but a few rooms, and half of the largest room was sectioned off for a table where his bead jewelry was made.

Back in Vilcabamba, I didn't understand his operation. Here, I saw that his daughter, his niece, and his wife were full-time workers. They'd sit at that table for hours each day sticking a needle and thread through tiny beads. An unobstructed, high wattage bulb hung from the ceiling. It made for an interrogation-room feel.

Alice was a very casual woman of excellent Spanish. Her translation allowed some conversation between Angel's family members and us. But exchanges were lean, as his family was shy and studious. Angel, however, wasn't shy. He was proud to show off their work. He pulled another table out to display the totality of their ability. There were necklaces, bracelets, and more insect-shaped jewelry.

He surprised me with a perfectly shaped, green frog. He had made several, and I bought two. Alice purchased a large amount of his jewelry. He was happy to have the business. And I thought it was incredible the day I gave my mom that little frog that had traveled from Saraguro, Ecuador, back to West Virginia. She hung it from the rearview mirror of her car.

Visiting Angel was but a brief stop. We caught the bus then traveled north eighty-five miles to the Azuay Province and Cuenca—Ecuador's third-largest city. Cuenca is highly recommended amongst American tourists. Sure, I'm not a city type. As such, I really wasn't there to engage in anything city people like to do. Instead, I wanted to verify, on my own accord, whether it felt anything like its reputation of being similar to a European city. I wanted to know if it felt safe.

Moreover, I wanted to feel the magnetism Cuenca has toward the expat. Foreign transplants regard Cuenca as the prime location to call home, should they move to Ecuador. The method I'd use to make observations was cramming as much site-seeing in as I could in a day and a half.

We arrived near sunset in Cuenca. I could barely draw an observation other than Cuenca looking like it sat in a giant natural bowl. Looking down into that bowl, the roofs were colored that bright, terracotta orange while mountains surrounded the city. Cuenca's sprawl fingered in each direction to the base of these mountains. From a bus window afar, it was a city painted in natural hues. Beige, whites, light browns, and brick reds stuck out to me. To the West, Cajas National Park showcased Andean ridges with a distinct tree line. The peaks' tops were grassy and smooth, unlike most I'd seen in Ecuador.

June lived in a brick apartment building that afforded a great view of Cuenca. It was near the Monte Sinai Hospital. We stayed there overnight. In the morning, a brilliant blue sky with puffy white clouds welcomed the day. The sun exposed the surrounding mountain glory. I was happy for a day of exploration. June's apartment was a three-quarter mile walk to the historic part of town. I'd start there. The evening before, she filled my head with Cuenca's must-sees.

Topping that list was old Cuenca—known for its concentration of centuries-old, Spanish-influenced buildings. Some, like Cuenca's Old Cathedral, were of the sixteenth century. The old city was designated as a UNESCO World Heritage Site in 1999. Following in the footsteps of Ecuador's capital city of Quito—the world's first city designated as a world heritage site—Cuenca is one of 1,121 such sites worldwide.

Many consider it the finest city in Ecuador. Foreigners transition smoothly here for its modern convenience, perceived safety, weather, and quality of life. With a population of 400,000 urban residents, it's neither too big nor too small. For many, Cuenca's just right.

I walked down a long median of grass toward the old city. A man on an ATV was bundled tight on the cool morning. He pulled into a fuel station. Right away, Cuenca was set apart from any American city. I thought, *Do that in the US, and you'll be fined.* A few steps further, and an Ecuadorian woman on the opposite side of the street, waved, saying, "Hola" to me. That was another immediate difference between America and Cuenca. Perhaps I stood out as a visitor. Whatever the case, it's nearly impossible to snag eye contact from a stranger passing on the same sidewalk in an American city, let alone on the other side of the street then have them greet you. The woman made me feel welcomed.

I continued on to a river crossing. Behind me, I'd

left an area of town no different than an urban scene in any modern society. There were wide paved streets, schools, hospitals, public transportation, and monuments to important figures. Right in front of me was a scene stuck in time by those who shaped block and concrete into buildings centuries ago. The Tomebamba River served as the border to the old city. I crossed its bridge and ascended a sharply curved hill into the world heritage site.

Where to go and what to expect when I got there was not much of a concern. I was being lured by the beacon of sky blue domes at Calderon Park five blocks ahead. The streets were narrower here. Most buildings weren't more than four stories tall. Many of them boasted long series of narrow and tall archways as part of covered walkways at street level. Matching the archways were round-topped windows with all matter of intricacies designed into their sills. Of the facade enhancements, the roofline moldings had been given great attention to detail during construction. Most were crafted to resemble multiple layers.

I imagined the masons of the time being more motivated by doing good work than pumping things out for progress. You just don't see many buildings with authentic, attractive, and often unnecessary veneers anymore. Nowadays, it's all for profit. If a stone is used in construction, it's likely a fake stone. I think the attraction of Old Cuenca can be found in the aged authenticity locked in the sight of the buildings. That's undoubtedly what I liked about the place.

Arriving in the town square showed me the largest town square I'd seen in Ecuador. This was Calderon

Park. Here, I found the building of the sky-blue domes. They belonged to the enormous Cathedral of Immaculate Conception. Locals called it the New Cathedral. An unsuspecting tourist, exactly like myself, would be quick to conclude that this giant church was also centuries old. However, its construction began in 1885 when the Old Cathedral could no longer handle Cuenca's growing population. The New Cathedral's footprint and height make it one of the largest structures in Cuenca. An enormous, arched entry of fifty-plus feet demands the eye. Meanwhile, those entering the cathedral look like diminutive, humanoid toys. That is, if you're at any sort of a distance from the building.

Around me, a city was on the go. On a street opposite the New Cathedral, I spontaneously decided to take a double-decker bus tour. *How can you beat that for seeing the city quickly?* As the bus moved carefully through the busy streets, I listened to the tour guide explain Cuenca in Spanish; then in English. This is how I discovered that the New Cathedral was new and that there was an Old Cathedral.

We drove along, and I took note that not all sections of Old Cuenca were historically treasured buildings. Once we were a half a dozen blocks from Calderon Square, Old Cuenca took on a look of what it predominantly is—residential housing and small businesses. There was an air that even these buildings were older than most of urban Cuenca. To spot rows of attached buildings with a generously colored mural on the end unit was rather common. Some of the homes were vacant and needed repair, while graffiti was as prolific as the murals. I took great pleasure in the murals.

The bus headed out of Old Cuenca, backtracking from the way I'd walked in. While cruising on a residential street, a visiting couple and I laughed at the surprise of low-hanging power lines. I could have literally stood up to change seats and been clotheslined by the wires. We were just fortunate not to do so. That's a supreme difference between traveling in the US and other places. Minor infrastructure matters like that are largely solved in the United States.

From here, I hadn't a clue where the bus would go. It moved along until we stopped at a location above town. We were at a parking area at the Church of Turi. The allure to this location was an overlook that displayed all of Cuenca. I could see the New Cathedral and the apartment building where we were staying. I could see the opposing mountain range and two rivers running below. The Andes owned the horizon from here. We were allowed some time to shop and eat. I did nothing more than wander the street and take photos.

When we returned to Calderon Park, I took off on foot. Cuenca had much more to see. June had told me to visit the flower market. She said it was one of the best in the world. I took her word for it and gave it a walk-through. It was only a block away at the rear of the New Cathedral. It sat in a space, perhaps the size of thirty parking spots. Florists displayed their flowers under large canvas umbrellas. I strolled through while carrying a supremely male perspective. I was indifferent and felt awkward being there.

At one of the displays, I asked the price for a dozen

roses. The woman replied, "Tres dolares." (Three dollars) Just then, I could see why many tourists would hold it to such acclaim. The floral variety was truly outstanding. Each color of the spectrum was represented by an equally diverse number of flower petal shapes. Sure, it wasn't one of those things that I'd seek out. But later, I'd find it was ranked as one of the world's top ten flower markets. That realization made it pretty cool to me.

In another display of color, the streets around Calderon Park were a ruckus. A parade was making its way through. Musicians were playing brass instruments on foot. Trucks had been fashioned into floats and absolutely smothered with fine, colored lace and blankets. Sometimes, even the windshields were covered with lace. There were teenage girls riding horses and wearing dresses of layered lace, so long, in some instances, that it nearly covered their entire horse. The horses themselves had colorful blankets draped over them. Many of the floats had a single child sitting in the back in a royalty-like theme. At least, that's how my foreign eyes saw it. There were balloons and dancers and folks in suits walking along. The parade was colorful, and the spirits of those involved, even more so.

I continued around. A street vendor was selling tamals. I bought two for $1.50 and took a seat. Tamals are often bits of chicken wrapped in thick dough and cooked in a banana leaf. They're about eight inches long and shaped like a soft taco. There are a hundred ways to make them. On this day, mine were chicken. One takes it upon themselves to eat unregulated street food. I have never been above it. The price was perfect.

Just after the tamals, I found an odd dessert at another vendor. A young lady was selling what looked like ice cream. Her cart was topped with a cutting board and piled on that was a mountain of ice cream. Or so I thought. I noticed folks walking away with cones, yet she didn't have a melting mess on her hands. I approached and asked for one. She grabbed a cone and used it to scoop into the pile. I quickly saw she was scooping some sort of colored whipped cream. It tasted like whip cream but much sweeter. I gave her a dollar for two.

I chewed on them cluelessly. Was it a whipped cone? Was it whipped at all? Was it even dairy? I didn't know. I just knew it had sugar in it. So, it went down the hatch. Curiosity forced me to know the answer later. These cones were espumilla or sweet mousse. Espumillas are made with egg whites, gelatin, fruit pulp, and sugar. I could have eaten a dozen.

Nowhere in the day did I feel unsafe, nor did I spot alarming things like razor wire. I'd traveled enough on foot to make my feet hurt. From block to block, and through poorer-looking neighborhoods, no one bothered me. I cruised through tight markets, where folks were selling shoes and clothing, and I didn't fear pickpocketing. I openly filmed without much more than a look from anyone. If anything, people's eyeballs took notice of my odd feet. I was wearing sandals, and there's no part of my body whiter than my feet skin. A group of girls even passed by giggling about it. I took it in stride. Roaming Cuenca was a solid experience. Yet, I hoped to find one thing before we left the city.

Back at June's, I had an odd, super craving for

pizza. In Vilcabamba, I couldn't find a New York slice like I enjoyed. Cuenca was big enough to probably have two or three pizza joints that could craft a fine slice. I asked June if she knew of anything local. She did. There was a place a few blocks from her apartment called Tuttu Matto Pizzeria. I set off.

Inside, it was as if I stepped into an Italian slice of New York City. There were green, white, and red columns, red and green chairs, red brick walls, and giant posters of the Statue of Liberty. American music was playing. I ordered a small pepperoni pizza and took a seat. Just like on the bus from Guayaquil, my ears bathed in the vibration of American tunes that were sung in English.

The Eagles, *Hotel California,* played as I took my first couple bites. It could have been angels with harps playing, and I'd have known no difference. My country's political and social environments may have been taking confusing turns, but the music, thank God for the music. I missed it.

Two friends and a Redemption

I'm not sure what makes Vilcabamba most notable. It may be its reputation for being the valley of longevity, word of mouth by world travelers for its way of life, or Mandango—the sleeping Inca. A rock formation stands high above Vilcabamba. If you're looking at it lengthwise at just the right angle, the side profile of a human head is nearly impossible to mistake. If you take a closer look and apply a little more imagination, you can make out crossed arms in the chest area. I knew of Mandango since day one in Ecuador. But it wasn't until February 1, 2017, that I'd explore Mandango entirely by chance.

    I hadn't done much since returning to Vilcabamba, but that was the point. I wanted no more than to exist as a foreigner as normally as possible for three months. My near-daily, low-key mission was to travel to town, eat something, take notice of lifestyle differences, meet folks, and try to enjoy the experience. If I really needed an excuse for not doing more, I was down to less than $150. Extensive travel was out of the question. Besides, how do you really get to know a place, and where you stand in it, if you keep moving?

It was about eleven a.m. when I took the bus from the farm to Vilcabamba. I'd found a favorite restaurant in town that I frequented for the price of their food and its portion size. For $3.50, you could get stuffed eating shrimp and rice, with a drink and a side. I called it my maintenance meal. Eating healthy on the farm had helped me to drastically lose weight. I was a literal stick man. This carb-heavy maintenance meal kept me alive twice a week and allowed some basic socializing.

On this particular day, I ordered my usual. A gal was sitting at the adjacent table alone. In this situation, I often activate the introvert within, go deep in my head while hoping women will talk to me. But there was something either in the air or the shrimp that day. I said hello to her, and she replied back eagerly. The conversation ping-ponged so smooth from there that I didn't even remember eating. *How lucky am I*, I thought.

Her name was Sandrina. She was an Indonesian woman, six months into her travels in South America, and it was her birthday. She had been as far south as the Atacama Desert. The rest of her time had been spent roaming about the Andes free-spiritedly. She was new in town. I was eager to hang out with someone other than Boring Man, my alter ego. The conversation led to Mandango. Hiking it seemed like the right thing to do, so we went for it.

Neither one of us was prepared. My shoes were at Vilcabamba's town cobbler for fixing. I was wearing cheap sandals. Sandrina had stretchy pants, a full stomach, and the will to hike with a stranger. Many people that have met me quickly find that I'm too polite for my own good—a quintessential nice guy. And, boy, do the stories of rejection go deep in my life because of my nice nature. Sandrina didn't say it, but I'm sure she perceived no threat from me.

Neither one of us knew where the trailhead was, but I had a rough idea. Vilcabamba was hardly larger than five blocks from its town center in any direction. Word on the street was that the trail began on one of those final blocks. Naturally, we'd look for it going uphill. Finding it was pretty easy, albeit weird in the sense that it felt like going through someone's lawn. This sparked a memory of an unconfirmed rumor I'd heard of a tourist being robbed and stabbed on the trail the year before. I kept an alertness about me that I tried to hide from Sandrina with smiles. Once we passed the last house, my mood calmed.

Hiking forward became pretty fun. Sandrina had a great sense of humor and a carefree attitude that helped erase my lameness. The borders she had crossed, the giant mountains she had seen, and her experiences thus far placed hiking Mandango as a walk in the park. For me, heading up the trail felt long overdue. I wondered how it took me two months to do so. Internally, the answer was apprehension for going alone. Externally, I had contacted one of Vilcabamba's expats, who'd hiked it many times. But he became difficult to reach after agreeing to hike with me.

We passed through a scrubby bit of forest. In one bend in the trail, a huge cow caused us to pause. Its enormous size and the one-way-in, one-way-out scenario forced us to try to get it to move. It wouldn't. So, we eased around.

The trail left the forest for an open, brushy hillside. Straight ahead, it wandered back and forth gently. Then, it became a section of short and sharp zigzags like Homer Simpson's hair. Those sharp back and forths meant we were coming up to a really steep climb. As the elevation increased, the mountain kind of swooped up to prove so. Around us, none of the plants were tall. We could see the way to the base of Mandango clearly, minus one short section.

Sandrina led. She was a couple years older, a bit shorter, and I had solid legs from running daily. Her pace was the appropriate one at which to climb. When we came to that short section we couldn't see, things began to get fun. The trail was so steep that, for thirty yards, you could reach straight ahead and use your hands to climb like an animal. Someone had built a rail here, but it was worn and flimsy. Sure, a fall wasn't certain death, but now we were high enough to feel like we'd made it to the sky. Here, the trail was of loose gravel and slippery. There was very little to grab onto, giving us a sense that we were out in the wide open. Our steps were careful and short until we rounded the first peak.

This was the halfway point. To make it there, we earned a breather. Filling our lungs was matched with exhales of awe. The surrounding mountains encompassed tiny Vilcabamba like a cradle. And they were spectacular from here! I could see five ridge lines toward the horizon. Spinning a circle further, I could see the ridge where the farm was—five miles away. Just out of sight was the bed and breakfast at which I was staying.

Our gaze turned to a somewhat surprising cross tiled with mirrors. It stood about ten feet tall. On the way up the hill, I saw a man looking at it and fixing his hair. I thought that was strange. From anywhere but right beside it, it looked like a cross painted white. There were many afternoons in Vilcabamba where I looked at it and assumed it was white. I never caught a reflection to urge me to think otherwise.

This cross was central to the lore of Mandango. To the Inca, this geologic formation was a sleeping giant—a god lying down with a mission to protect the Valley of Longevity from earthquakes and natural disasters. Ecuador is known for these natural phenomena. It's part of the Pacific's ring of fire. Incan legend says Mandango was in a war with another mountain. Giant stones were thrown between them. Placing the cross settled the giants and stopped the ground from thundering. One could assume the thunderous ground as being earthquakes and volcano eruptions.

From here, we were able to see proportion expand right before our eyes. Mandango suddenly went from looking like it was fifty feet tall and three hundred feet long, from the streets of Vilcabamba, to one hundred fifty feet tall and eight hundred feet long. Intimidation and beauty equalized in the giant formation. I could understand why the Inca looked at it so. Its walls were sheer. Nothing in the valley stood out as an anomaly quite like Mandango. A question inside me, and I know many before me, was, "How did it get like that?" I wanted to get closer.

Sandrina surprised me when she submitted to staying at the halfway point. She didn't want to go further. I couldn't understand why. Many words of encouragement were bounced right back at me with a smile and her honest reply of, "I'm tired." This was a bummer. There it was, 500 feet away, and she didn't want to climb it. We'd already committed an hour to hiking. She was so close!

She agreed to chill out until I got back. There was no way I wasn't going for it. I set off on a trail that led straight to Mandango. When I was about fifty feet away, a lot of things became apparent. Mandango was perfectly vertical at ninety degrees. It was alarmingly tall. But it wasn't a rock formation. No sir, it was weirder than that.

The walls of the entire formation looked of sand and mud sedimentary deposits where one could imagine an ocean floor being lifted by tectonic forces during the creation of the Andes. Then, with erosion, severe in this case, the soft walls had chipped and fell off, tiny bits at a time. There were no mega-sized rocks involved. An accurate observation is that Mandango looks like 100-plus feet of seafloor mud, speckled to the hilt with round river rocks and eroded by water. The round rocks poked out like pimples from the, now supremely hardened, mud and sand. Each rock seemed as if it was waiting its turn to fall off the mountain and leave a little pocket of emptiness. Like discovering the cross being covered in mirrors, I was just as surprised to find that Mandango wasn't just a big ol' brown rock.

I continued around the rear of Mandango, an area that's not visible from Vilcabamba. Given my complete lack of knowledge of the trail, I didn't know how far I'd go before ascending to the top. Behind the formation, it was supremely quiet. It was a type of quiet I'd felt on a windless day in the desert of West Texas once. Other than my footsteps and breath, there wasn't a sound. The formation blocked all incoming wind. And the silence increased the feeling of solitude.

Here, the trail tightly paralleled Mandango. To my left was a sheer cliff, while to the right was a valley with a depth of a thousand-plus feet and a hillside that would be difficult to stop rolling down. The trail itself was pretty easy to follow, albeit tough on the ankles. It was more angled than flat.

I found a left turn in the trail among a small patch of trees. After a short and muddy climb, I was on the upper portion of Mandango. Up here, there were only grasses. It gave the giant head-shaped formation a hint of hair, if you will. I walked no more than fifty feet further and was stopped by my own good sense.

The trail continued but in a super precarious fashion. To my left was an eighty-foot vertical fall. To my right was a wall of grass, easily at an angle not safely climbable. Straight ahead, the trail had eroded, thereby creating a dip for about twelve feet that was on the very edge of the cliff. I could see how the trail had been breaking away. Given that I was in sandals with wet feet, and there was nothing on which I could grasp, I didn't continue. My imagination got the best of me, and I could see two things happening. One, the trail breaks free the moment I step on it, or my foot slides out of my sandal, and I slip off the cliff. I was disgusted with myself and disappointed to make this decision. I felt like a pussy.

Hiking back to Sandrina, I couldn't shake that I failed the mission. Sure, I was happy to not have fallen. But would I really come to Vilcabamba and not summit Mandango? I didn't know. Sandrina asked if I had made it, noting she didn't see me up there. I told her, "No." Then, I blamed it on my wet sandals more than the trail breaking free. It was something burning inside me at that point.

She was positive, with a hint of neutral. She had other things on her mind. She made a friend in the hour that I had been gone. She introduced me to a fella named Lex. He was a year into traveling South America from his native Australia. Lex was a couple years younger than us. We had noticed him sitting by himself, writing or drawing something in a notepad earlier. Between the three of us, we hit it off so well that we planned to hike to a waterfall I'd heard of the next day.

Lex left us to climb Mandago. I told him of what I learned about the trail and wished him a safe climb. He was wearing sturdy boots. Sandrina and I left the mountain and parted ways for the evening. I looked forward to hiking with both of them the next day.

When we met again, it was afternoon. We were in great spirits. Their company, and our similar ages, really made my day before we even began walking. I did almost everything alone during my time in Vilcabamba. Alice and Dan had been there for nine years, and to them, nothing was as new or as exciting as it was to me.

Their age also made them seek less strenuous activities. Sandrina and Lex were the closest I had come to having friends in Vilcabamba.

I told them where I thought the trailhead was for the waterfall. They followed me without question. I was with two completely free spirits. We began the hike on the edge of town. A gravel road led us up a hill but then became nothing. It was a dead end. Intuition kicked in about ten minutes too late. We were going the wrong way. We backtracked to a road and went a little further away from town.

Vilcabamba was phenomenally pretty through here. The folks who called this part of town home had really gone out of their way to create flower gardens, creative-looking dwellings, and finished homesteads. Tall and mature eucalyptus trees grew between the road we walked and the fast-flowing Yambala River. A mountain ridge made a brilliant green and almost natural triangle. It was a hillside steeper than any I had noticed around town. The walk was as enjoyable as a neighborhood walk could be. The lingering feeling that I was walking in California surfaced again. It really looked like a Californian neighborhood.

We knew we were on course when a sign read, "Parque Nacional Podocarpus." It displayed a camera, hiker, and waterfall emblems. The trail began with a walk bridge crossing the Yambala. Within five minutes, we were treading through landscape changes that seemed too abrupt to make sense.

Immediately, the trail was steep and wet. Our footing was speckled with deep, muddy indentations made by horse hooves. On either side of us, earthen, vertical walls were often higher than our head height. This made for a feeling of hiking through a narrow tunnel. Perpetual shadows had combined with heavy foliage to keep moisture in the ground. A bit of humidity rose from the mud. We were going uphill quickly and sweating.

In a couple hundred yards, we'd come out of there to a new environment. It was almost like being in the desert. Green, thick-leaved plants that looked like sun rays were plentiful here. Beneath our feet were bone-dry stones. The grasses looked dry, and we had an open vantage point ahead. Not far along, and again, we were in another channel. This one was far over our heads, maybe twelve feet high. Coarse and loose, dry stone made for its walls. It zigged and zagged to create an air of fun, like walking through a maze. I didn't know why this trail had these narrow channels, but I guessed the horse traffic helped speed the erosion. I'd never hiked anything like it. I was glad my new friends got to experience this novelty too.

The further we went from town, the more it felt like wilderness. Of course, we weren't way out there. A look around, and you'd see hills roll to the horizon ahead and behind. Vilcabamba was hidden in one of their valleys, while the waterfall was in another. We passed through wet and dry spots several times. If a section of trail was forested, it would be muddy. If open, the sun had baked it arid.

A couple folks passed us while riding on horses. We got to see how much quicker the horses could climb. We were in terrain that allowed them to walk twice as fast as us. It seemed like we were only going uphill. In these higher elevations, Spanish moss hung from trees. That was another surprise.

Through the couple miles to the waterfall, I learned of the travels that my two companions had had, as well as places they recommended seeing. They told me where they were headed next and of the people they'd met. I had to stick their recommendations into another storage file in my mind. I didn't tell them how pathetically broke I was.

We reached another crossing of the Yambala. By any stretch, it was a creek of fifteen feet wide instead of a river. We heard the waterfall crashing nearby, and the trail had emptied into a pasture. Two cows stood calmly at an adobe lean-to. We followed the sound of the water while descending through their pasture. On the far end, a treacherously steep and muddy trail was the way to the waterfall. Toward the bottom, it was so steep and slick that a rope had been installed to help folks descend.

We had found a secret world at the base of the waterfall. The tiny Yambala, that we crossed only minutes before, now rumbled after its eighty-foot drop into a shallow pool. Rock walls enclosed the sides of the waterfall. Growing from them was a hyper-green moss. The wind from the falling water was forceful enough to have the rock walls look alive as the moss fluttered ceaselessly.

We took our shoes off and waded in. Then I took my shirt off and introduced my two tan friends to the color West Virginia white. I didn't care for forgiveness. Shyness wasn't necessary. This was a special moment with good people. The waterfall was freezing cold. Lex took a series of pictures showing me trying to catch my breath instead of smiling under the falls. We enjoyed lunch and each other's company in a brief moment of perfection.

Heading back to Vilcabamba was much the same as hiking to the waterfall. Somehow, it felt like we were going uphill the whole way. Reality showed us that we'd climb a mountainside, descend a bit, climb again, and descend further. Regardless the climbs were steep. I joked that Ecuador must be the place where all of the old-timers went to school. Many folks grew up hearing the story, "When I was a child, I walked to school uphill, both ways." On the waterfall hike, we found that sensation.

We grabbed a taxi at the trailhead, hopped in the back, and rode to Vilcabamba. I talked them into going to a place called Charlito's. Over a couple beers and a lot of laughs, I got to appreciate the time spent with Sandrina and Lex. The next day, they'd be leaving Vilcabamba. I'd likely never see them again, and I'd miss them.

The story of the waterfall could've ended there. But a few days later, I returned alone. I had discovered that I only took photos when I was there. I didn't record a second of video, and I wanted to do so. This was a perfect reason to reengage with the waterfall. I looked forward to experiencing the neat channels in the trail and being in the backcountry again. I looked forward to filming the hike there, the waterfall itself, and feeling redeemed.

When I arrived at the waterfall, no one was there. For an hour, I had it to myself. Peace on Earth; that's what it felt like. On the way out, I looked at the beautiful waterfall and said, "Adios cascada." (Goodbye waterfall) I'm pretty sure I'll never see it again. On the way back to Vilcabamba, I slipped and fell down twice in the loose rocks on the trail. If only Sandrina and Lex could have seen that!

Still, something was eating at me. I was nearing the two-week mark for leaving Ecuador. I hadn't stepped foot on top of Mandango. A beautiful morning graced the Loja Province on February 13, 2017. I had my shoes back from the town cobbler, and, by golly, I was going to conquer Mandango.

My comfort for being in Ecuador was now at a level where I felt safe everywhere. So instead of taking the bus into town, I decided to walk the five miles and then hike. There was but one issue. If I could make it past an ornery white dog two miles up the road from the farm, I'd be home free. That sucker had chased me and nearly bit my calf while jogging one day. I left the farm with a walking stick. I was ready for him.

Fortunately, the dog didn't hear me walk by. Instead, I stumbled upon a dozen cows being ushered down the road to a different pasture. I matched their pace for a half mile, loving the simple, rural life. A couple smooth miles after that, and I was at the base of Mandango, looking up.

My feet strongly marched to the part of the trail where I'd given up before. Then, I realized it still didn't seem safe with shoes. There was no way, in hell, that I would turn back. Carefully, I took a step forward. The trail's lean angle favored falling off the cliff. I shuffled a little further. My body was kept close to the grass wall.

My thought was, *Hold together, dirt. Hold together.* It did.

I moved on through a trail in the grass that wound back and forth. Mandango's top was like a smooth dome of grass. The terrain was just steep enough that walking straight to the top would be asking for it. One slip, and there would be no chance of recovery.

Part of the trail was wet with a natural spring. This increased the odds of a slip and made not a lick of sense to me. Mandango was a projection of Earth the way a table is a projection from the floor. Respectively, it's not all that large compared to the surrounding mountains. *How did the water get forced up here?* Mandango seemed too narrow for that. I spoke about things going uphill in Ecuador. Apparently, the water does, too. I still can't understand it.

Moving onward, I carefully followed the trail, thinking of that spring. Then, there it was, the top of Mandango. In a moment of sweet redemption, I had made it. I took out my pocketknife and scratched Sandrina's name in the soil. Then, I took a picture of it to share with her someday. On our hike to the waterfall, Lex had told me he'd made it to the top of Mandago. He got to see what I was now seeing.

Allowing my body to spin a circle made for a 361-degree view of some of the most remarkable terrain one can hope to see. The extra degree was added in my hillbilly math for experiencing another place in this wonderful country, where whatever you hope to find, you're shown that and a little bit more.

Carnival

I'm an observant fella, albeit with limitations. When I'm engaged in a moment, it has my full attention. Things that immediately surround me are always highly considered. If they're important, then they're acknowledged. If not, they're rapidly dismissed. Hardly anything goes unnoticed.

The same cannot be said for the attention allotted to planning ahead. I'm too easygoing in that aspect. I'm not much for pushing the issue, being nosy, or salty to others. I don't need to be the center of attention. In the immediacy of conversation, I usually listen rather than lead. I don't often know what people are up to in their private lives, and I don't usually know what a community has planned. In all, I just appreciate it when things are working smoothly. This general way of being meant that Vilcabamba was about to teach me something new and exciting that I never saw coming.

Alice and Dan very much lived American-style lives in Ecuador. They were homebodies who kept an umbilical-like attachment to their native world through the internet. Dan's Spanish was only marginally better than mine after these couple of months. They were folks who had a good, peaceful existence in a foreign country that they influenced positively. They employed three men, focused on recycling, composting, growing their own food, and sharing smiles with people when they happened to come around. But they weren't the type to engage culturally with Ecuador.

Our conversations were mainly about science, art, the food we'd eat, their travels, lessons learned, and especially, the current political environment. President Trump's election was a hot topic at the farm. Any mention of Vilcabamba preparing for a massive celebration called Carnival was fleeting and flanked by indifference. My friends failed to share just how ransacked Vilcabamba would become with visiting Ecuadorians. Those details came slowly, as subtle surprises, through daily observation.

I was still going to town nearly every day. Often, I'd just go and not even let my friends know. The truth was, I was pretty lonely at the farm. I spent most of my time at the B&B listening to music, writing, exercising, or sitting on the deck looking at the view. I had stared at the glorious mountain, across the way, for hours upon hours. I came to realize that daily trips to Vilcabamba could help combat loneliness. Sometimes, I'd walk there. Sometimes, I'd take the bus. I had a routine and looked forward to those brief trips into town.

One day in late February, I was eating the same old

shrimp and rice that I always had. Nothing was out of the ordinary. There were always about three people walking in the town square, and the sun was almost always shining. But right beside my adopted restaurant were a few black crates and some metal framing left in the road. I thought maybe a store was relocating or someone was moving. Nothing more occurred to me.

The next day, I was back again. Some guys had erected a stage. They had emptied those crates to add a roof to the aluminum framing. I noticed speakers and microphone equipment. *Okay. Vilcabamba's going to have a play.* This looked like the kind of stage used in Macas on New Year's Eve. Still, the scope of things didn't hit me. And I said nothing to Alice and Dan. Two more days passed. The weekend was drawing near. Vilcabamba was now hosting twice the town's population. Carnival was a buzzword on the street.

Being observant does not mean you're always slick. These changes should have been a clue for the coming days. I learned that, what the Ecuadorians were calling Carnival, was the same celebration that I knew as Mardi Gras. I'd been to New Orleans's Mardi Gras three times. I knew it was a wild ride. I knew that you could trade beads for boobs and that beer was buy-one-get-one whether you wanted two or not. I knew that Mardi Gras was at the end of February. And I even knew that a thing called Carnival was celebrated in Trinidad. Hell, I even knew that it was like Mardi Gras. But I never made the connection that most of Latin America celebrates Mardi Gras and calls it Carnival. And it certainly never occurred to me that peaceful Vilcabamba would be a hot spot for it.

Another truth is, I'd never been a religious person. Carnival is a celebration in line with Christian traditions. The only Christian holidays that affect my life are Thanksgiving and Christmas. If it weren't for my family acting on them, they'd pass by as just another day. All of it is lost on me. One could argue that I'd been lost too. However, I did know I'd welcome the chance to celebrate with the townfolk before Lent. Excitement grew inside me when I realized what was coming.

The long, silent, yet beautiful days at the farm would be over for a while. Keeping up with the changes kept me on my toes. Carnival was so new and coming so fast. I now had more to do than just going to town to write notes, eat, and look around. Going forward, I stayed in town most of the daylight hours from Friday until Fat Tuesday.

When the weekend of Carnival came, the town was overtaken. Its sleepy existence was no longer. Children were running like packs of coyotes. They were swimming and splashing in the fountain of which I admired. Vilcabamba was throwing a way bigger party than I imagined. Hot damn!

There was a parade celebrating local groups of school children, town elders, and new residents. These groups organized synchronized dance routines. Judges were stationed along the parade route to pick a winner. At no time in life had I seen a group of elders boogying down so continuously. They were going with every bit of steam they had. A few cars were outfitted as floats and decorated wildly. Ecuador's military participated in the parade by playing instruments. A few locals showed off their horsemanship through riding displays.

The stage from a few days ago was now alive with music and dancers. It hosted a swimsuit competition. The nature of the women participating seemed so reserved that I perceived them as too shy to do such a thing. It lacked the outrageous flaunting you might see at a place like Panama City, Florida, during spring break. Beyond that, there were wild costumes and a boy-band group that the young locals seemed to enjoy. A rock band kicked it for a while. The crowd went a little nutty then. In moments of downtime on the stage, we were lathered in bumping party music from those speakers. I could hardly believe what I was seeing, given nearly three months of being there.

It wasn't until Monday that things ramped up really strong. That's when the town was at full capacity and spilling into the streets. Now, Vilcabamba was hosting thousands. I couldn't grasp just how many. The little mountain paradise had become an erratic ant farm of a town. I learned a few things pretty quick. You'd better have your head on a swivel, and you better not wear clothes that were easily ruined.

Ecuador's Carnival brought with it a fantastic tradition of war with water guns and assault by spray foam. For a foreigner, this part of the festival was most shocking. I could imagine some of the older expats being intimidated by the volume of splashed water and spray foam to the face.

In fact, some expats had expressed as much. A few of them even suggested I skip the festivities based on their personal, and somewhat holier-than-thou, opinions of Carnival. This was a time when the tiny village of Vilcabamba didn't work for the desires of many of the retired foreigners now calling it home. Instead, Vilcabamba hosted the desires of the Ecuadorians. Carnival was being celebrated as a Christian tradition in a town of primarily Catholic followers. The expats were the odd people out. Some seemed selfishly offended over Vilcabamba's temporary condition. In fairness, I must mention that there were a handful of familiar foreign faces participating. I was happy to see them embracing a tradition of their adopted land.

I'm absolutely wired for just such a thing as Carnival. Number one, I like to party. Number two, I like to take honest fun to the extremes. In all of my childhood, there was never a water gun fight like the one Vilcabamba was hosting. Every dang kid had something with which he or she could squirt you in the eye. And if they didn't, they'd find a bucket. And if it wasn't a kid pouring water on you, it was their parents or their aunts and uncles. The fountain was taking a licking, given the sheer number of buckets draining it. I saw one group of young men carrying their buddy to the fountain to toss him in. Getting wet, being wet, and especially making others wet was the name of the game.

If the squirts weren't coming from a water gun, then they were coming from a spray foam can. Vendors were roaming around selling cans of foam for two dollars. I doubled up for a chance to have one in each hand. Folks sprayed me, and I sprayed them back. It didn't matter if they engaged me or if they were innocent. I even watched a cop take a water balloon to the head without incident. It was so culturally accepted that no one fussed. And the spray foam didn't ruin my clothes.

Fat Tuesday arrived. By the afternoon, the town was at it again. The water gun fight seemingly never ended. Foam was still flying, and people were speckled white everywhere you looked. Food vendors offered what they'd uniquely brought to Vilcabamba. I walked over to Charlito's to build up some steam before putting my party legs on. Unwisely, I brought my backpack with my laptop and camera to do some writing and filming.

Before Carnival, I'd come to frequent Charlito's about once a week. The American fella, who owned the place, was a decent man. At Charlito's, you could grab a bite to eat and have a cocktail. A person of an English tongue could talk to another person who spoke the same. His patrons were older foreigners. I started to see familiar faces there. I liked the place.

Now, I'd finished writing and wanted to get out and about. But I had my backpack. I asked the owner if I could put it behind his bar for a couple hours. Nothing about him said that this was something to worry about. I trusted him. He agreed. I ordered a whiskey and coke and asked if it was okay to take it outside the bar. He said, "Sure. Just bring my glass back." I agreed, and off I went—to party.

I left Charlito's gripping a glass full of ornery. Walking the town square, with the other hand holding a can of spray foam, I spotted a fella named Cesar. Yesterday, I'd met Cesar for the first time when he approached me. I suppose he wanted to see what I thought of Carnival. He was an English-speaking Ecuadorian who'd traveled solo from Loja. I thought Cesar was dressed too well for the occasion. His hair was long and slicked straight back. He was calm, in nature, and clean-shaven. In the entirety of being around Cesar, he never took off his oversized fancy sunglasses. He operated smoothly, just like a mafia guy. I would have never approached him first, given his apparel and serious facial mug.

Now, I'd found him again. He was happy to see me. And we both knew that we had a buddy to celebrate with. I was all about continuing the water fight, and Cesar just played along. He didn't participate, but he wasn't immune to being a victim, even in his nice clothes.

When my glass was dry, we'd walk it back to Charlito's for a refill. This was possibly the worst thing for a guy like me. In the States, things are so regulated as to often take the fun out of them. The fact that I could leave the bar with a drink meant that I didn't have to miss anything. I was able to enjoy all of the music. We met all kinds of people, and I could not have been having a better time. Unlike my experience at New Orleans's Mardi Gras, Carnival here felt safe. I was happy.

By dusk, Charlito's had served me enough alcohol to beer-goggle three people. I was handling it finely. Drinking and not losing total control was a skill gained through years of practice. Nearing midnight, we'd had enough of the town square and the water fight stuff. Cesar asked if I'd like to walk to a bar down the street. I didn't know there was a bar in the area of Vilcabamba he mentioned. I thought that everything was residential there. He said he had been there before during Carnival. It was an Ecuadorian hangout. He said it was like a dance club. He encouraged me, "Girls will be there."

Hearing that, I needed little convincing.

We arrived at some sort of scuffle in the parking lot. Even in my drunken state, this drew a red flag. I knew I'd stand out in the crowd. The booze urged me to play it cool as I followed Cesar inside. Right away, we noticed the girls weren't as plentiful as we'd hoped. I hit the dance floor anyway. I'd been known to shake a leg in the past. And nothing quicker than whiskey could spur it. Hell, I thought I might lure in a female if I showed 'em my liquor moves. I'm not saying they're good, but they're unique and a whole lot better than that stiff and sober dancing I did during Christmas at Iliana's family home.

Cesar stayed off to the side. He was fine with a drink and a steady head bob to the music. It was the perfect move for a guy wearing sunglasses in a dark dance club. I gyrated for a few songs and then ordered the finalizer cocktail. I should have stopped at the whiskeys from Charlito's.

We had been there for an unknown stretch of time when I started noticing folks looking at me. And not in a friendly way. I was being sized up by some of the young men. I hadn't done anything threatening to anyone. But I did stick out as the only gringo in there. I was experiencing what happens when folks allow the alcohol to take hold of the controls.

Liquor is referred to as spirits, quite accurately. I've found that negative energies sometimes become free to roam after too much to drink. Under their control, the body is just along for the ride. Whether it's a social problem or a wicked hangover, alcohol nearly always comes to collect payment for the fun.

And it had gotten me again. I came to the edge of being sick while consuming the finalizer. The unwelcome I could feel from a few drunk Ecuadorians merged with my nausea. And so, I did the smart thing. I just walked out the door. Ten minutes before, I thought I might party until the sun shines. Now, I had to figure out where to go. The buses weren't running this late. Taxis weren't around either. And, I didn't have a room in Vilcabamba. The only option I could muster was walking back to the farm. So, off I went.

The choice to leave the club was one born of a perception of things happening in a highly drunken state. I mentioned before only having one potentially negative engagement with Ecuadorians. That occurred when I was at the New Year's celebration in Macas. In absolute fairness, I may have read the signs wrong on this night at the club, and the young Ecuadorian men may not have been sizing me up. Something told me they were, though. Instinct urged me to leave and to stifle the possibility of a truly negative engagement with Ecuadorians. That night, as I exited the club, I moved into the territory of not having a single negative, face-to-face engagement directed toward me by Ecuadorians in the entire three months. This is an important truth for travelers wanting to visit Ecuador.

Earlier, when we walked into the dance club, we had already shaved a few blocks off the distance to the farm. Now, as I passed through the edge of town, things weren't so bad. There were pole lights and lights coming from residences. Once I was out of town, it was much the same with a little less light. I was fine in my drunken stumble. I made it to the turn that I'd follow to the farm. Everything was fine. There were four and a half miles to go. I'd done this walk several times in the daylight.

Walking in the dark, however, was a different story. A mile into the walk, the thought of being overtaken by the drunk locals at the bar grew traction in my brain. I picked up the pace. I couldn't have put myself in a more vulnerable position to come up missing. I was in a place where those things could pass like water under the bridge. The scenario played in my head—men role up in a truck behind me, they jump out, overtake me with numbers, and I wind up as bite-sized fish snacks.

Two more miles down this supremely dark and rural road, and the thought of being overtaken by others was overtaken by the thought of the jaguar. I knew that darn thing was out there somewhere. But where? This thought completely took over. Soon, my brain sizzled with fear. I took my pocket knife out and opened it. My right hand held it firmly, and I picked up my pace even more. As I looked around, the only light came from the slim selection of stars in the sky. This section of road was sparsely populated with homesteads. In between each, my eyes struggled to see the pavement beneath my feet.

I was a mile from the farm when I discovered just how dark the road was. My knife was out, and I simply didn't want to die from that jaguar. Anxiety owned me. The alcohol seemed an afterthought. And it sure as hell didn't make me braver. I was walking at a fast pace when my body was enveloped instantly by something big. I nearly screamed. The dark was so thick that I couldn't see that a fallen tree had blocked the road. I walked straight into a mess of branches at a fast pace without seeing any of it. My arms were hanging by my side. If it had been the jaguar, I stood no chance of seeing it coming. Four miles of walking did nothing to adjust my eyes to how black the road was.

I backed up and out of the branches. I felt somewhat of a relief in how funny that would've looked to a bystander. I climbed over the tree, giggling at myself for being so helpless. The farm was a few turns away. I could nearly see its lights.

Making it there didn't alleviate the anxiety. It surprisingly increased it. I left the sure-footedness of the road surface for the trail to the B&B. I crossed the walk bridge and prayed for 300 more feet of luck. I was headed to the exact place I'd heard the jaguar each time. To get there, I'd have to pass through shin-high grass, a banana grove, and to the edge of the forest. I stepped forward since it was the only choice.

Relief was immeasurable as I closed the door behind me. I was acutely aware of just how stupid that walk was. Exhaustion overwhelmed me when the anxiety dissipated. I'd ran so high on adrenaline that I didn't realize I was still drunk.

In the late morning, I panicked upon remembering that I'd forgotten my backpack at Charlito's. There was a couple thousand dollars worth of electronics in there. I took the bus to Vilcabamba with my fingers crossed. The owner of Charlito's had stored my backpack in the back safely. Doing me that favor makes me proud to mention just how honest of a man he was and how highly I recommend patronizing his establishment if you'd pass through.

Vilcabamba was now reset to the peacefulness I'd come to know. Workers were cleaning things up. Folks were steadily leaving. There had been a rapid transformation made in the village. It was quiet again.

The Carnival celebration's timing felt like I had come to Ecuador and lived peacefully and happily for three months. In return, a farewell party had come to town. Of course, it would've happened whether I was there or not. But Carnival felt sent from above. I didn't know of its qualities, and all of it was a surprise. To me, it further strengthened the benchmark of unity expressed among Ecuadorians. There was no way to thank them all for the party. So, I say it now. Thank you all for the party!

Three Months as a Foreigner

I found another level to being a foreigner on the day I ran out of money. Carnival came to town and picked my pocket dry of the last bit of change to my measly name. I neither make apologies, nor do I regret what I'd done. But I admit it was irresponsible to buy drinks, food, and spray foam and have a good time. Even less wise was traveling to South America with $579. In a few days, I'd fly home. I was in a pinch and needed some money.

Whenever we need money in life, we can rest assured that providing value to others is a way to earn it. I approached Alice with my financial issue. Surely, there was something I could do around the farm to provide her value. She came up with something on the spot. The lower field, located near the B&B, needed weedeating. And there was an old access road, leading to the far end of the property, that needed the same treatment. She agreed to pay me for that service.

I thought, *Great! I can earn a couple hundred bucks to travel home with.* But this is where I discovered that unforeseen *extra* level to being foreign. Alice plainly said that she'd pay me twenty dollars in American money for eight hours of work. This is also where the fool in me got what he justly deserved. She was dead-on in her analysis of the situation. I needed money, and she had money. But she also employed three full-time workers who'd normally weedeat. Why did I expect to be paid American wages when they would do it for Ecuadorian wages equaling about twenty American dollars a day? I found that, until you face this sort of thing, it's not apparent. I had to work as a foreigner rather than as an American. With the time I had, I could leave Ecuador with sixty dollars. I set to weedeating.

Those three days passed. Alice intuited that I should have a little more travel money. She sweetened the pot when she came up with the idea of paying me to make short videos to be shared on the web. These would showcase her building lots for sale. Years before, she cleared and leveled land in an adjacent field in hopes of attracting buyers who'd want to build and be part of an organic expat community. As of then, none had been sold. My job was to film the lots in the best light possible while editing text into the videos. She agreed to pay me $100 for this. Video editing requires considerable time, and I was out of time. So, we agreed that I'd do this in the States. Then, I would send her the final product.

Three months in Ecuador showed me innumerable differences in where I was and from where I had come.

During the weedeating, I realized that the farm wasn't home to a lawnmower. I learned that I hadn't seen a lawnmower in three months. They didn't seem to be a thing in Ecuador. Instead, machetes and weedeaters were the observed tools for trimming and cutting grass.

In three months, I didn't lay eyes on a single, white egg. Nor did I eat a refrigerated egg. In the States, we pasteurize eggs and then refrigerate them. That's mostly unnecessary. I would go to the market in Vilcabamba and buy three dozen large brown eggs for three dollars. I'd leave the eggs on top of the B&B's refrigerator in defiance of the norm. Those eggs, coupled with rice, and free fruit and vegetables grown at the property, were my main diet.

I left the United States weighing 201 pounds. The diet in Ecuador had been so effective that my body thanked me by dropping twenty-seven pounds. About two weeks before I left Ecuador, there was a day when I was sitting on a park bench in Vilcabamba. All of a sudden, I noticed how thin my legs had become. I'd not seen anything more than my face in a mirror for three months and didn't have access to a scale. It wasn't until I returned home that I'd find my new weight of 174 pounds.

Life had become sticky notes of scribbled highlights. On day forty-nine, I was sitting on that same park bench when two foreign backpackers walked through Vilcabamba's central square. They took notice of the fountain and the Catholic church. They were smiling at the quaintness of the village they'd just entered. Their necks were rubberized, and their eyes were sponges of observation. Their backpacks were fully filled. Both had their elbows bent tightly so that their hands held the backpack straps to comfortably help support the weight. They were a young couple out exploring the world.

As they walked about, both held a semi-lost look on their faces. My thought was, *I once walked through just like them, looking equally as impressed and lost.* How perfect it was of them to be making their memories together. There's no doubt that, to someone out there, these two were their Sandrina and Lex.

Day forty-nine also showed me a rather scary side of foreign life. Alice, Dan, and I had dinner together. After dinner, I walked down the hill to my room in the dark. Often, I'd lay down and edit video in the bed or read a book. As I was lying there, a storm began brewing in my stomach. Diarrhea was on the way. I jumped out of bed and rushed to the toilet. It escaped violently from me. Afterward, I looked down, and the bowl was filled with blood.

My knees weakened. My vision diminished. Then I passed out altogether and woke up just before I hit the floor. This caused my knee to smack the tile while my arms fought for stability. A trait of my being is to become nauseous and pass out easily. I wish it wasn't so. The blood in the toilet overwhelmed me so much that I knew there was a big problem inside my body.

When I was composed enough to walk steadily, I went back to Alice's bungalow to seek advice. There, I learned that if you develop a problem throughout the night, you have to live with it until the doctor arrives at the hospital in the morning. According to Alice, Vilcabamba's hospital was closed. She didn't own a car, and none of us had cell phones that would work. It was determined that I should stay with them overnight, just in case. They offered some cushions as a bed, and I slept on the floor.

In the morning, I again had diarrhea. This time, the color was normal. Overnight, I became sick with lethargy and headaches. That lasted two days and then cleared. I have no idea what happened and consider myself lucky.

Luck was on my side again when I awoke one morning and slipped my socks and shoes on. While walking downstairs with coffee on my mind, I noticed my right shoe feeling a little more snug than usual. My head was groggy and still waking up. That tired indifference allowed my toes to investigate the lump in my shoes. My middle toes slid across it and poked at it. They messed with it while I made the coffee. Once I had the cup filled, I headed upstairs. I was convinced that something was going on more than a fold in my sock.

Then a thought hit me. There's a huge spider in my shoe! A memory of being a teen, where this exact thing happened, startled me to full alertness. In that encounter, I naively took my shoe off and reached in, not knowing it was a giant wolf spider. The spider felt like it could have been a piece of crumpled paper. When I opened my hand, the spider spread out. I nearly died on the spot! I learned a tremendous lesson, then. Never reach in!

On this morning, I knew what to do. Take other measures. I slipped my shoe off and tapped it on the floor with the opening facing down. Sure enough, a chunky scorpion came blazing out. I cringed as the nerves were excited on my skin from head to toe. The scorpion made a break for a crack in the wall. I used the same shoe to send him to his maker. I was lucky to have not been stung.

Southern Ecuador showed me a land of few rodents and sparse insects. I found most of my insect interactions in the evenings when I'd help Dan cut fruit for dinner. At the farm, there was no use of pesticides. If a mango had a couple larvae, we'd cut around them and move on with life. There's no way I can say that without mentioning how disgusted it made me when I first arrived there. By three months, it was an afterthought. A man's gotta eat.

And when a man eats a worm, it's usually on accident. One day, I was casually eating a sapote fruit, holding it like an apple and had half of it ingested. Just before I took another bite, I looked down to see a small worm. The odds are that I ate a couple that day. It still haunts me a little.

The lessons matched the observations, and both compiled to create a full experience. Three months in a foreign land can show you so much or fail to show you things at all. There wasn't a single time that I saw a plane in the sky while in Southern Ecuador. I didn't see a single US penny despite half of the change in my pocket being American. All American money was accepted except pennies. And it wasn't uncommon to find an Ecuadorian coin with rust on it. I always found that bizarre.

Milk jugs were nonexistent, too. Instead, bags of milk were sold at the stores and markets. In three months, I didn't make a phone call. Nor did I see a tanked water heater. Each one had been tankless. And most were hooked right to the shower spout to make a bulky contraption hanging in the shower.

Something as benign as toilet paper could also be rare. During my travels, there wasn't a public restroom stall stocked with toilet paper when I desperately needed it. Fortunately, on all but one occasion, I was carrying napkins. Learning to do so came early one afternoon at Vilcabamba's bus terminal. I was forced to use my underwear as toilet paper then. Once I exited the stall and walked outside, I immediately noticed a woman selling toilet paper at the restrooms' entrance. I'd unwittingly walked past her minutes before. For ten cents, she'd supply a person with enough paper for a few hearty wipes. I had taken toilet paper for granted.

During a spell where I was having trouble sleeping, I went to town for something like NyQuil. Vilcabamba's pharmacy offered sleeping pills called Zopiclone. I tried one and had a good night's sleep. Then I tried two and slept even better. I'd never found anything that helped me fall asleep faster. Then a week went by, and I'd sleep all night. I'd then awaken with the side effect of grogginess throughout the day. This spurred me to look into what I was taking.

Zopiclone was a controlled substance in the United States because of its addictive qualities. It worked by tranquilizing the central nervous system. Doing so meant the sleep cycle was being altered. Between the groggy days, the potency, and the US's classification, I decided it wasn't for me. Yet, the experience of more freely available drugs opened my eyes wider to the world.

In the purest form of surprise, it became apparent that Ecuadorians absolutely love volleyball. My first taste of this came on the first day there, when I noticed a volleyball court near the farm's walk bridge. That court was usually packed on the weekends with men in highly competitive matches. As I'd stand at the bus stop, I'd watch them athletically keep a volley going with bodies that weren't as athletically in sync. I'd hear shouts and cheers. The men were serious enough that I'd bet there was money on the line. If not for their supreme mastery of the game, I surely would've loved to join. My height was good, but they didn't need a roadblock hindering their efforts. And just as bizarrely, it was happening among the most rural of settings.

Walking around Vilcabamba had shown me numerous backyards outfitted with volleyball courts. Often, when I'd leave town to return to the farm, I'd walk to the furthest bus stop just to watch a game of volleyball being played. It was a constant. I appreciated their ability from across the street. After all, I'd never seen any competent volleyball matches in person. They were really good—even if some of them sported beer bellies.

I came to know the phenomena later as Ecuavoley. Their version has a few unique qualities. They use three players per side. Often they use a soccer ball, a higher net, and the ball can be held upon receiving it if it's less than one second. Since I'm no expert, I must leave it there.

There was another time, sitting at that same bus stop, when I watched from afar as a driver worked on his broken-down car. For twenty minutes, I waited for the bus and watched as ninety percent of the vehicles leaving Vilcabamba pulled over to offer the stranded driver help. I couldn't believe my eyes. Values were more alive here than anywhere I had ever been.

We were existing in a place that seemed like another time or an alternate reality. Taking a plane to Ecuador never allowed me a sense of how far I had traveled. In 2011, I rode my motorcycle from West Virginia to California. I could feel the distance and the country's size through all those miles ridden. In the case of being in Ecuador, I never felt I had traveled just as far from home. Flying took an aspect of adventure out of the experience.

I was in a land where people looked different, where they spoke a different language, where the hills were larger and shaped differently, and cultural intricacies were countless. Flying from home to South America, the change was too sudden. It felt nothing like driving from the East Coast to the West Coast and watching as the Appalachians flatten into the Great Plains. There was no emotion like seeing the Rockies on the horizon or feeling the emptiness of the vast desert. Absent was the excitement of the rise and fall of the West's other ranges to the edge of the Pacific. Flying to the next continent south felt much duller and strange, though the distance was an equal 3000 miles. In Ecuador, I couldn't shake the feeling that I'd popped through a wormhole to Oz.

Other weird revelations came from the experience. Some time of reflection showed me that it's possible to be from two places at once. There's no need to pick a side unless you desire to stifle yourself. Undoubtedly, I was an American man. I had positive character traits and notable flaws because of this. These made me who I had become. But I learned that being one hundred percent American left out positive character traits worth adopting. The main one being, the unflinching hospitality shown by Lucia and her family. It's entirely possible to go above and beyond for an extended period of time for someone you enjoy or love. Americans have moved away from this and are becoming more insular. For those that have permanently relocated to Ecuador, I hope they've adopted some of the good stuff. Alice and Dan surely had by letting me stay for three months.

Depending on a person's values, Vilcabamba had what the modest would call endless good stuff. I saw it everywhere. I saw it in the small things. One day, I was having coffee at a restaurant near the town square. The corner of this building made one corner of an intersection. The restaurant had two wide side doors. One door faced one street. The other door faced the adjacent street. These doors were always wide open during business hours.

I was sitting inside with my laptop open when a wiry brown dog walked through the restaurant. His head moved back and forth to make eye contact with the humans at the tables on either side of him. Though he couldn't verbalize what he wanted, I heard him loud and clear. He was saying, *Anybody selling scraps? I'm buying. How about you, lady? How about you, white guy? I'll pay ya by letting you pet me and looking cute. Just throw me a little on the floor.*

He strolled without stopping. No one fed him. I only had coffee to offer. He never looked discouraged. He had all the charm of a New York City paperboy from ages ago. His passing through was like hearing those young men yelling the headlines at passersby. That's the little things. I was tickled with it. Dogs aren't allowed those privileges in the US.

Sundays were my favorite days in town. When church would let out, Vilcabamba's town square reflected the idealism of Mayberry. Children were free to go where they pleased to play with their friends. They'd be running around holding oranges as snacks instead of candy bars. Their parents leisurely chatted and caught up. A man with a soft-serve ice cream machine filled cones for fifty cents. The skies were often blue and peaceful and matched the lack of urgency in getting through life. I always looked forward to handing that man fifty cents, getting an ice cream cone, and watching an innocent scene to which I was foreign. I could imagine movie directors trying to capture scenes like this in the childhood coming-of-age films with which I grew up. Here those scenes were happening in real life. I appreciated it so.

The little things were practically everywhere. Alice's farmhands had become my friends over the three months. She would meet with them each morning for their day's assignment. Given the size of the property, there was always something to do. I'd see them regularly walk by the B&B with their machetes, or they'd be carrying buckets for harvesting. Sometimes they'd have shovels in hand. The men tackled each day with smiles and humility. They were some of the most genuine folks I met.

In my earliest days there, I barely understood their role. Moreover, I was highly unnerved by them constantly carrying machetes. Movies are likely responsible for this instinctual reaction to machetes as weapons rather than tools. I'm somewhat ashamed to admit that I kept my distance in the early on. One morning, Alice took the time to introduce me to the guys. From then on, I'd throw a hand up at them to wave and say, "¡Buenos dias!" (Good morning) They'd always reply with a cheerful, "Buenos dias."

After three months, my Spanish was solid enough to have a basic conversation. One afternoon, one of the men spent his half-hour lunch break sitting at the B&B with me. Our conversation never stopped. I got to know him a bit better and learn about his interests. He was a father first. He liked shoes from America. He wanted to be sure that I liked his country. When I'd struggle with language, he'd say, "Tranquilo, Mike." (Relax) It meant that there was no judgment. He expected nothing more than a little time to sit with a buddy. My American side sought perfection in my words. It was unnecessary. His reminder toward me was a reminder of the little things.

Tranquilo, chevere, and chuta became words I adopted for their repetitious use by the folks I met. The days with Lucia gave me chevere and chuta. To the American ear, chevere sounds exactly like Chevrolet. Yet, it translates to cool, as in, "You got new shoes! Cool!" While traveling with Lucia, there were times when I thought, *Why does she keep saying 'Chevrolet?'* Thankfully, she said chevere more than chuta. Chuta translates to crap, as in, "We missed our exit! Crap!" Both of those words survived as words I'd use back in the States. Especially, chuta.

The adoption of the phrase, Que tenga un buen dia,

served me over and over. It means, have a good day. It was a friendly escape when I was lost in language. Inexplicably, the phrase stuck to my brain. It simply never faded from memory. It was the first solid sentence I could say confidently. Its message is positive no matter where you're at in a conversation. I used it when I could no longer keep up to initiate the end of a conversation. I focused on using it politely. I'd say it as I looked someone in the eye. I found it the perfect phrase for wishing someone well, even though I could no longer communicate. They were left knowing my intentions were good.

I'd highly recommend learning this phrase in the respective language of the country anyone chooses to visit. It will serve you well. Learning only how to say phrases that serve your travel needs often leads to confusion, as answers can vary based on who's responding.

I used "Que tenga un buen dia" many times while engaging one of Vilcambamba's residents. She was a female a couple years older than me. She took an interest that I perceived as genuine at first. She looked me up on Facebook and would ask when I was coming to town again. I'd respond via an online translator. We'd meet in the town square. The conversation would always dead-end at, "Que tenga un buen dia." She always spoke so fast that I couldn't keep up. It was rapid-fire. She never grasped that, if she'd slow her speech down, I might keep up. I even asked, in Spanish, if she could slow down. After clunky attempts at conversation, I'd smile, give her my patented phrase, and set off.

Later, I found her interest to not be genuine. I was back in the States a couple weeks when she messaged me to ask where I was. She hadn't seen me in a while. I told her I was in West Virginia. She became upset. She said, "You were supposed to take me with you." This, I had not gathered at all. I guess those were the words she was firing at me all along. She also said, "I wanted to marry you for a green card." I told her, "I'd never marry outside of love." That's the last I heard from her.

One evening, Alice told me a great story that highlighted the integrity of the Ecuadorians—even when they are off track. She said that shortly after moving to her property, a local man, and an accomplice, broke into her house while she was home. They demanded money, mistakenly thinking Alice was wealthy. She was fast on her feet when she said, "Dan, go get my pistol!" Then she told the men, "I was an expert shot back in America." While Dan wasn't handling it so smoothly, he did play along. The men didn't advance due to this warning. It gave Alice time to play on their deeply held faith. She said, "For this, you'll be punished in Hell." The youngest of the men freaked out and left. He believed her. His religious conviction was that strong. A gun was never produced, as Alice didn't own a gun. The other man left shortly after without harm toward either party. Ecuadorians are fine people at heart. That's the little things.

In time, I'd come to know the answer to whether or not the rich land around Vilcabamba could provide a longer life. The answer lies in a different question. Can living in the Andes, in and around Vilcabamba, provide a better quality of life? The answer soundly is yes. I was a lab rat for finding the answer.

The decade before my arrival, I battled alcoholism. I ate horribly and was regularly overweight for my thin frame. Alcohol was just as available in Ecuador as it was at home. However, there's something that happens when a person is exposed to a peaceful, balanced existence in a beautiful place. They find that it's awfully hard on the survival of their vices. It had never been so easy to be sober.

The Shuar gave me alcohol in their chicha. At Christmas, I was offered a tiny cup of warm wine, mistaking it for water. On day eleven, I drank a beer to ease up. I had been a nervous wreck. Then I enjoyed two beers with Lex and Sandrina. The evening hanging with Cesar at Carnival was the only proper boozing I experienced in Ecuador. Being this sober was a change I couldn't see coming, yet I needed it all along.

Ecuador was so good to me. I was sad the day I had to leave. Morning arrived with a goodbye to my friends. I hugged Dan and Alice and shared sincere handshakes, along with well-wishes with the farmhands. Those guys were doing stonework in a culvert for the day. They'd be so privileged to remain in a place I came to believe as an Andean wonderland. As I walked from the farm, I knew I'd miss everybody.

I caught the bus to Vilcabamba. There, I caught the next bus to Loja. An hour and a half after that, I was sitting on a plane in Catamayo. While flying to Quito from Catamayo, the last person in Ecuador I met was a man named Luis. We spoke in English as he sat with me. He was a traveling salesman. Everything about him radiated humility. I was lost in the thought that the first person I met in Ecuador was a man named Luis in Quito's airport, three months before. Talking to the first Luis took the edge off in the moment. Speaking with this Luis took my mind off of how I wasn't looking forward to going home. I told him of my adventures, and he told me of his travels. We were instant friends, just like so many I had already met along the way. Undoubtedly, if a person travels to Ecuador without a friend there, they'll have one before leaving.

From Quito, I flew to Houston. Two young American guys sat beside me in the seats. They were pals of one another, and they were different than me. I hoped for conversation but overhearing theirs cemented that they'd have no interest in what I had to say. Everything about them was of a shallow, materialist mentality. In five hours of flying, we didn't exchange words.

Houston's airport was a land of cold shoulders and dodging eye contact. I felt like I was in a machine. The infrastructure was perfect. Things were clean. Floors were shiny. Nothing had a do-it-yourself look, like many of the buildings of my past three months. I noticed no flaw in Houston's airport. Instead, I noticed something about the people. I felt like I was surrounded by a bunch of androids. I was back in the land of scarce affability.

I had just spent months in a culture that recognized my existence. I had been around women who'd greet me with a hug and a kiss on each cheek. The men would shake my hand, look me in the eye, and smile. It sucked to be just a number again.

Arriving at Dulles International, in Northern Virginia, brought me back to a world of even less affability. For the first time in months, I was in freezing temperatures. My folks were happy to see me and more shocked to see how thin I was. My mom said I looked like I was starving. Really, I'd never been healthier. On the drive home, I felt as though nothing had changed except myself.

Their concerns were of an American nature. They entailed their demanding jobs, their sometimes-strained relationships with others, and the cold of winter. It was impossible to express the vividness of Ecuador, the colors I'd seen, the beautiful traditions, or the perfect temperatures. No amount of eagerness to share my stories would be enough to convince others to appreciate the things I'd seen as much as I did. It became clear early on that I'd have to lock down this memory.

A great distaste for my home's cultural momentum came in the clarity of observation on my first day back. I was in a store in West Virginia and standing in a checkout line. The young woman in front of me was not paying attention to the clerk. The clerk tried multiple times to call her. The young woman was absorbed in the actions of her unruly, obese child so thoroughly that those of us in line were forced to bear her ignorance as she fought with her kid about which giant candy bar he could have. When she'd ignored the clerk calling "Ma'am" for the third or fourth time, I went around her. I figured she wasn't ready to check out.

She snapped her attention to me and said, in blatant unawareness of her own ignorance, "It's my turn. Some people are so ignorant." Though I love the United States dearly, I could not have felt sadder for my country. We're becoming dangerously overweight, like the young mother and child. We're outrageously self-centered and distracted. Our families are falling apart, and we're lonely. What's more, is that we embrace ignorance and use it to lift up tribalism. Materialism has its claws sewn into our souls as much as our digital screens now own our eyes. This young mother had already lost herself in all of it. Her child didn't stand a chance.

I submitted to the young mother. She paid for her things ahead of me. I paid for mine, then walked to my car with an image in my head of a toddler I'd seen two days before. It was one of beautiful evening sunshine glowing through the windows of the bus I was riding. A few rows in front of me, the toddler was standing in her seat and with her hands pressed against the window. She balanced herself as she looked out. Then, she looked back at me. Her clear and clean, big brown eyes were as precious as gold. Outside the bus, the greens glowed brilliantly in the light of the low sun. The bus came to a halt. It was her stop. Her mother gathered her gently, and they left.

The bus continued through the winding curves and brilliance of the evening light toward the farm. I rode along, still entranced by Vilcabamba's mountains as much as the day I arrived. In a corner where the low sun shone perfectly on the window, where she had stood, I saw two tiny handprints glow with the colors of the rainbow from the bit of oil left by her hands. She'd left her mark. And as I sat in my car, I felt grateful for having known a place where folks haven't lost their way and one so beautiful that it left its mark on me.

If you enjoyed this book and want to check out another one by the author, please have a look at *132 Days* on Amazon.com

www.ingramcontent.com/pod-product-compliance
Lightning Source LLC
LaVergne TN
LVHW041613070426
835507LV00008B/219